Table of Contents

Practice Test #1

Practice Questions

1. Which three classes of lymphocytes circulate in the bloodstream?
    a. Cytotoxic T cells, stromal cells, and plasma cells
    b. B cells, NK cells, and stromal cells
    c. Cytotoxic T cells, helper T cells, and suppressor T cells
    d. Thymus-dependent T cells, bone marrow-derived B cells, and natural killer cells

2. When friction is applied to the skin, it increases the dissipation of heat by approximately ___.
    a. 60%
    b. 75%
    c. 80%
    d. 95%

3. What is the primary function of antidiuretic hormone (ADH)?
    a. It stimulates cell growth and replication.
    b. It increases production of melanocytes in the skin.
    c. It decreases the amount of water lost from the kidneys.
    d. It stimulates smooth muscle contractions in the wall of the uterus.

4. A synovial joint that allows one bone to rotate around the surface of another bone is called a(an):
    a. gliding joint.
    b. pivot joint.
    c. saddle joint.
    d. ellipsoid joint.

5. In cross-fiber friction, the direction of the stroke is applied:
    a. transversely.
    b. longitudinally.
    c. circularly.
    d. medially.

6. Which of the following is NOT a form of depression?
    a. Bipolar disorder
    b. Posttraumatic stress disorder
    c. Seasonal affective disorder
    d. Dysthymic disorder

7. Which is the best definition of wellness?
    a. A measure of how healthy an individual is.
    b. A response to being healthful.
    c. Behaviors and habits that have a positive influence on health.
    d. Behaviors that positively affect health.

8. How many phalanges do each of the second through fifth toes contain?
   a. 1
   b. 2
   c. 3
   d. 4

9. Which type of data is obtained through assessment by palpation?
   a. Objective
   b. Subjective
   c. Neither
   d. Both

10. Which muscles of the forearm make up the "wad of three?"
   a. Brachioradialis, extensor carpi radialis longus, extensor carpi radialis brevis
   b. Extensor indicis, extensor digitorum, extensor retinaculum
   c. Brachioradialis, anconeus, extensor carpi ulnaris
   d. Extensor carpi ulnaris, extensor digitorum, extensor digiti minimi

11. A client is experiencing pain related to exacerbation of rheumatoid arthritis and has requested a massage. Is massage during this period safe for the client?
   a. Yes, as long as the client communicates her level of pain tolerance.
   b. Yes, because gentle massage can reduce stress and provide comfort.
   c. No, massage will worsen any inflammation during this period.
   d. No, massage is not safe for individuals with RA either during symptom exacerbation or remission.

12. Which of the following is NOT an example of dry heat?
   a. Heating pad
   b. Infrared radiation
   c. Microwave
   d. Sauna

13. Which cranial nerve innervates the lateral rectus muscle?
   a. Abducens
   b. Oculomotor
   c. Vestibulocochlear
   d. Vagus

14. Which phase is part of mitosis?
   a. G1 phase
   b. G2 phase
   c. S phase
   d. Metaphase

15. Which of the following is a way to personalize the connection between a therapist and a client?
   a. Maintaining eye contact
   b. Using the client's name
   c. Listening attentively during the consultation
   d. All of the above

16. What is "touch for health?"
    a. Another term for massage
    b. A form of applied kinesiology
    c. A specific type of passive touch
    d. A program developed out of structural integration

17. The action of the pectoralis major muscle is:
    a. adduction and flexion at the shoulder.
    b. flexion, adduction, and medial rotation at the shoulder.
    c. extension, adduction, and medial rotation at the shoulder.
    d. depression and protraction of the shoulder.

18. At which step in the contraction cycle does the power stroke occur?
    a. The formation of cross-bridges
    b. The detachment of cross-bridges
    c. The pivoting of myosin heads
    d. The reactivation of myosin heads

19. Which of the following are classified as types of pain responses?
    a. Psychological and physical
    b. Physiological and physical
    c. Psychological and physiological
    d. Physical and anatomical

20. Which of the following involves protrusion of the nucleus pulposus through a tear in the annulus fibrosus?
    a. Slipped disc
    b. Ruptured disc
    c. Herniated disc
    d. Bulging disc

21. A(n) _____ contraction occurs when the peak tension developed in a muscle is less than the load and the muscle elongates.
    a. concentric
    b. eccentric
    c. isometric
    d. egocentric

22. When writing a SOAP note, what information should be included in the "objective" portion?
    a. Techniques used during the session and any changes in the client's symptoms.
    b. Suggestions for future sessions.
    c. Information gathered by the therapist during history taking, observation, and interview.
    d. Anything the client tells the therapist.

23. What is the most appropriate massage to be done on an area affected by lymphedema?
    a. Superficial friction
    b. Lymph drainage
    c. Derivative massage
    d. Passive touch

24. Friction is being applied ____ if the movement is in the same direction of the blood flow in the veins.
    a. centripetally
    b. centrifugally
    c. distally
    d. proximally

25. How long can you apply friction to dry skin?
    a. 3-6 minutes
    b. 4-7 minutes
    c. 5-8 minutes
    d. 6-9 minutes

26. Which of the following is an example of an effect of massage on the muscular system?
    a. Heightens blood circulation to the skin.
    b. Favorably influences organs of the body.
    c. Increases activity of sudoriferous and sebaceous glands.
    d. Positively affects the range of motion of limbs that have limited range due to tissue injury.

27. What is NOT included in the marketing portion of a business plan?
    a. Clarified differential advantage
    b. Risk assessment
    c. Competition analysis
    d. Budget

28. Which of the following is a therapeutic application of deep kneading?
    a. Relieving the cold that arises from spasms of the small vessels.
    b. Promoting absorption in instances of serous effusion into the pleural cavity.
    c. Increasing weak muscles in size and firmness.
    d. A and B.

29. Which of the following components of bone is made up of outer fibrous and inner cellular layers?
    a. Canaliculi
    b. Periosteum
    c. Matrix
    d. Osteocytes

30. How much of your work time should be invested in marketing?
    a. 25%
    b. 20%
    c. 15%
    d. 10%

31. Which of the following statements best describes collagen fibers?
    a. They permit stretching and then recoil to their original length.
    b. They resist stretching but are easily bent or twisted.
    c. They do not permit stretching but will recoil to original length.
    d. They resist stretching and are not easily bent or twisted.

32. There is evidence that massage was employed by the Chinese as early as _____ years ago.
    a. 2000
    b. 2500
    c. 3000
    d. 3500

33. The kidneys rely on three distinct processes to perform their functions. They are:
    a. diffusion, osmosis, and carrier-mediated transport.
    b. filtration, reabsorption, and secretion.
    c. absorption, secretion, and reabsorption.
    d. filtration, collection, and channel-mediated diffusion.

34. Wellness is often represented as an equilateral triangle with three aspects that a wellness-oriented person strives to attain. Those three sides that the wellness model depicts are:
    a. psychological, mental, and mindful.
    b. emotions, attitude, and spirit.
    c. conditions, situations, and practices.
    d. physical, psychological/mental, and attitude/emotional.

35. What does light stroking do?
    a. Causes a contraction of the blood vessels
    b. Hastens the flow of blood through the superficial veins
    c. Enhances lymph flow
    d. Dilates the capillaries

36. Which of the following is a reason why it can be challenging for therapists to give high-quality therapeutic massage in a spa setting?
    a. Low expectations from spa guests
    b. Time constraints
    c. Inexperienced clients who have not formed an appreciation for bodywork
    d. All of the above

37. Which explanation best describes the first metatarsal?
    a. It is long and slender
    b. Its dorsal and medial sides are deep and difficult to palpate
    c. It articulates with the medial cuneiform
    d. It is an attachment site for the peroneus brevis

38. Kyphosis is an exaggerated curvature of:
    a. the cervical spine.
    b. the thoracic spine.
    c. the lumbar spine.
    d. each portion of the spine at once.

39. When preparing stones for a hot stone massage, water in the heating container should be kept between which temperatures?
    a. 100° and 130°F
    b. 110° and 140°F
    c. 120° and 150°F
    d. 130° and 160°F

40. In pétrissage, the muscles should be lifted from the bone or underlying tissue from what point?
    a. The point of insertion
    b. The point of origin
    c. The most lateral point
    d. The most proximal point

41. What does a release of information form contain?
    a. The client's name and the therapist's name
    b. The client's name and the name of the person(s) the information is being given to
    c. The client's name and the time frame in which the information may be released
    d. The client's name, the therapist's name, the name of the person(s) the information is being given to, and the time frame in which the information may be released

42. Which type of gland secretes the "fight or flight" hormones?
    a. Pituitary
    b. Adrenal
    c. Exocrine
    d. Endocrine

43. What is pathology?
    a. The study of viruses
    b. The study of disease
    c. The study of pain
    d. The study of structure

44. Contraindications that require the practitioner to adjust the massage when there are health concerns that render certain techniques inadvisable are called:
    a. regional contraindications.
    b. conditional contraindications.
    c. partial contraindications.
    d. absolute contraindications.

45. What is the Swedish system of massage primarily based on?
    a. Shiatsu, a finger pressure method
    b. Chi, the life force energy
    c. Western concepts of anatomy and physiology
    d. Various kinds of therapeutic baths

46. The vein and lymph channels are ____ in the vicinity of the ____.
    a. larger, joints
    b. smaller, joints
    c. larger, limbs
    d. smaller, limbs

47. Which kind of bath should be at a temperature of 90° to 94°F to stimulate circulation?
    a. Hot bath
    b. Warm bath
    c. Saline bath
    d. Tepid bath

48. Skeletal muscle is composed of all of the following except:
   a. fascia.
   b. nerves.
   c. osteocytes.
   d. blood vessels.

49. What role does a muscle play if it carries out an action?
   a. Agonist
   b. Synergist
   c. Antagonist
   d. Protagonist

50. Which technique can powerfully stimulate the nutrition of a joint?
   a. Beating
   b. Active touch
   c. Deep vibration
   d. Stretching

51. Which early advocate of massage discovered that sleep may be induced by gentle stroking?
   a. Hippocrates
   b. Asclepiads
   c. Herodicus
   d. Plutarch

52. Which of the following rules is false in regards to abdominal massage?
   a. General abdominal massage should not be administered until two hours after eating.
   b. The bladder should be emptied just before abdominal massage.
   c. Superficial movements should be avoided at first when working with a "ticklish" patient.
   d. Deep-kneading movements should be applied more quickly than for other parts of the body.

53. Which option includes the structures of concern for the endangerment site that is at the anterior triangle of the neck?
   a. Brachial plexus, subclavian artery, brachiocephalic vein, external jugular vein, and lymph nodes
   b. Axillary, median, musculocutaneous and ulnar nerves; axillary artery, axillary nerve, and lymph nerves
   c. Carotid artery, internal jugular vein, vagus nerve, and lymph nodes
   d. Median nerve, radial and ulnar arteries, and median cubital vein

54. Which gastrointestinal condition is characterized by abnormal muscular contractions?
   a. Crohn's disease
   b. Irritable bowel syndrome
   c. Ulcerative colitis
   d. Diverticulitis

55. What year was sports massage introduced into the Olympics?
   a. 1964
   b. 1974
   c. 1984
   d. 1994

56. What does "phagocytosis" literally mean?
    a. Cell drinking
    b. Cell eating
    c. Cell excreting
    d. Cell secreting

57. Which of the following is not an effect of the positive touch of massage?
    a. Lowered cortisol levels
    b. Lowered norepinephrine levels
    c. Lowered stress levels
    d. Lowered serotonin and dopamine levels

58. Is certification from a state or municipal regulating agency issued in the same way a license is issued?
    a. Yes, a certification and a license are the same thing.
    b. Yes, it just depends on what a particular state prefers to call it.
    c. No, a certification is not as valid as a license.
    d. No, a certification is awarded by schools, institutions, and professional organizations.

59. When is the observation portion of a client assessment?
    a. From the moment the client walks in the door until the client leaves.
    b. From when the initial interview begins to when it ends.
    c. From when the initial interview begins to when the treatment ends.
    d. From the moment the client walks in the door to the end of the initial interview.

60. What do beta-blockers do?
    a. Decrease blood pressure
    b. Affect heart rate
    c. Affect the strength of contractions
    d. All of the above

61. Which of the following is an example of someone who would be considered an independent contractor?
    a. A massage therapist who is told what fee to charge her clients.
    b. A massage therapist who performs her services under given guidelines.
    c. A massage therapist who is reimbursed for business and travel expenses.
    d. A massage therapist who is paid directly by her clients.

62. What is kinesiology?
    a. The scientific study of muscular activity and mechanics of body movement.
    b. The study of the structural and functional changes caused by disease.
    c. The study of the gross structure of the body.
    d. The science and study of the vital processes, mechanisms, and functions of an organ or system of organs.

63. To practice good ethics is to be concerned about all of the following except:
    a. the public welfare.
    b. your own welfare.
    c. the welfare of individual clients.
    d. the reputation of the profession you represent.

64. Which of the following is NOT a major fee-setting strategy?
    a. Setting a high price to target a small percentage of the population.
    b. Setting a price that competes with the going rate for the industry.
    c. Setting a lower price to gain a larger share of the market.
    d. All of the above are fee-setting strategies.

65. What does relationship-based marketing involve?
    a. Getting relatives to refer their friends and family to you.
    b. Getting clients to refer family members to you.
    c. Truly caring about your clients' welfare.
    d. Hiring a spouse for PR to help you expand your client base.

66. Who was the innovator of the seated massage, also referred to as chair massage?
    a. John Harvey Kellogg
    b. David Palmer
    c. William Harvey
    d. Elizabeth Dicke

67. Which of the following is NOT a major purpose for keeping client files?
    a. Future contact when in need of referrals
    b. Record keeping and the IRS
    c. Keeping well-informed of your client's needs
    d. Insurance reimbursement

68. Pain described as "persistent or intermittent over a long period of time, often dull and diffused" is what type of pain?
    a. Referred
    b. Subtle
    c. Acute
    d. Chronic

69. Which type of end feel is due to the stretch of fibrous tissue as the joint reaches the extent of its range of motion?
    a. Taut end feel
    b. Springy end feel
    c. Hard end feel
    d. Soft end feel

70. Does a client ever sign an informed consent after the initial consultation?
    a. No, just during the initial consultation.
    b. No, in some places it is not even necessary.
    c. Yes, after every few sessions.
    d. Yes, when an updated plan is created.

71. Which of the following is a non-steroidal anti-inflammatory drug (NSAID)?
    a. Naproxen
    b. Celecoxib
    c. Cortisone
    d. Both A and B

72. If a client tries to sexualize a therapy session, is it appropriate to terminate the session?
    a. Yes, you should walk out without saying anything.
    b. Yes, but you should still plan on maintaining the therapeutic relationship.
    c. Yes, ask the client to dress and leave, then promptly leave the room.
    d. Yes, state that you are uncomfortable, ask the client to dress and leave, and then promptly leave the room.

73. What is innervation?
    a. The distribution of nerves to a region or organ.
    b. A response to stimulation by sensory neurons that are normally inactive.
    c. The synaptic surface where neurotransmitter release occurs.
    d. The reflex in which interneurons are interposed between the sensory fiber and the motor neuron(s).

74. Which of the following types of cancer originates in epithelial tissue?
    a. Sarcoma
    b. Lymphoma
    c. Myeloma
    d. Carcinoma

75. Which business name is the best example for establishing a good reputation?
    a. "Smitty's Massage Parlor"
    b. "Smith Massage Clinic"
    c. Neither A nor B.
    d. Both A and B.

76. If your business plan is going to be used to secure a loan, what additional information should be added that is not otherwise included?
    a. Cover page
    b. Table of contents
    c. Appendix
    d. References

77. Is it a national requirement for massage therapists to be licensed in the United States?
    a. No, only the continental United States.
    b. No, it varies from state to state.
    c. Yes, but the license requirements vary from state to state.
    d. Yes, all the license requirements are the same in each state.

78. In which of the four major client-interview stages do you discuss the client's general issues and expectations?
    a. The initiation stage
    b. The exploration stage
    c. The planning stage
    d. The closing stage

79. All of the following are disadvantages of sole proprietorship except:
    a. All business debts and liabilities are the personal responsibility of the owner.
    b. The therapist possesses the profits.
    c. The owner is responsible for all business aspects.
    d. It may be difficult to obtain financing and unlimited liability.

80. Which is the correct order of the four-part method for resolving an ethical dilemma?
    a. Clarify the problem, identify the problem, describe what action should be taken, identify who should take action.
    b. Identify the problem, clarify the problem, describe what action should be taken, identify who should take action.
    c. Identify who should take action, identify the problem, clarify the problem, describe what action should be taken.
    d. Identify who should take action, identify the problem, describe what action should be taken, clarify the problem.

81. What type of barrier is the first sign of resistance to movement as tissue is manipulated through its range of motion?
    a. Soft tissue barrier
    b. Resistive barrier
    c. Physiologic barrier
    d. Anatomical barrier

82. A client is considered ____ during a massage session due to the inherent nature of the practitioner/client relationship.
    a. timid
    b. shy
    c. vulnerable
    d. quiet

83. How many hours after the injury occurred is local massage contraindicated for whiplash?
    a. 48
    b. 72
    c. 96
    d. Massage would be beneficial immediately following a whiplash injury.

84. Which structure contains densely packed myofibrils, large glycogen reserves, and relatively few mitochondria?
    a. White muscles
    b. Red muscles
    c. Fast fibers
    d. Slow fibers

85. Which of the following is classified as a diverse group of organisms that are potentially capable of causing disease?
    a. Cocci
    b. Bacilli
    c. Spirilla
    d. Fungi

86. An individual's scope of practice is directly related to ____.
    a. the skills she has gained and the training she has received.
    b. the rights and activities that are acceptable.
    c. the styles and techniques that she studied.
    d. whether or not she lives in a state that has adopted licensing regulations governing the practice of massage.

87. What does "interpersonal space" refer to?
    a. The actual space maintained between the client and practitioner during interactions before and after the massage.
    b. The space maintained between the client and practitioner during the actual massage.
    c. The amount of space present in any height differences between the client and the practitioner.
    d. The minimum amount of space required for a client to feel that the practitioner is being fully attentive.

88. Is it acceptable, as a massage therapist, to sell products in your business?
    a. Yes, you can sell anything.
    b. Yes, you can sell health care related products.
    c. No, you have to be a doctor, nutritionist, or herbologist.
    d. No, you're not allowed to sell products in a massage clinic setting.

89. Fibrous tissues that have tensions placed on them during muscular contractions are called:
    a. ligaments.
    b. cartilage.
    c. contractile tissues.
    d. striated muscle fibers.

90. Which of the following is NOT a reason to seek supervision?
    a. You experience feelings of exhaustion or burnout.
    b. Clients challenge your professional or personal boundaries.
    c. You change your regular care protocol for a particular client.
    d. None of the above.

91. Long, relaxing massages affect the autonomic nervous system by ____ the sympathetic nervous system and ____ the parasympathetic nervous system.
    a. stimulating, sedating
    b. sedating, stimulating
    c. stimulating, stimulating
    d. sedating, sedating

92. Which is NOT an example of a stimulating massage technique?
    a. Pétrissage
    b. Friction
    c. Percussion
    d. Vibration

93. Which of the following is essential to keep in mind about personal business cards?
    a. Keep a substantial quantity and always have some with you.
    b. Beauty is in simplicity of design.
    c. Convey major benefits in a quick glance.
    d. All of the above.

94. When assessing passive movement, pain and limitation in all directions generally indicate:
    a. bursitis.
    b. stretching of involved tissues.
    c. compressing of involved tissues.
    d. capsulitis.

95. All of the following are reasons that a license may be revoked, suspended, or canceled except:
    a. having a history of felony conviction.
    b. engaging in any act of prostitution.
    c. having too many speeding tickets in a certain amount of time.
    d. being guilty of fraudulent or deceptive advertising.

96. The resting tension in a skeletal muscle is called:
    a. muscle tone.
    b. muscle contraction.
    c. muscle tension.
    d. motor unit.

97. Which of the following correctly defines the acronym TART?
    a. Tautness, asymmetry, range of motion, tenderness
    b. Texture, asymmetry, range of motion, tenderness
    c. Tautness, active range of motion, range of motion, tenderness
    d. Texture, active range of motion, range of motion, tautness

98. In which of the four major client-interview stages do you create a vision with your client about his major goals?
    a. The initiation stage
    b. The exploration stage
    c. The planning stage
    d. The closure stage

99. Why are licenses and permits required?
    a. To raise revenue.
    b. To protect the health and safety of the public.
    c. Neither A nor B.
    d. Both A and B.

100. When a force is applied between the resistance and the fulcrum, which class of levers is it considered to be?
    a. First-class lever
    b. Second-class lever
    c. Third-class lever
    d. All of the above

101. In Swedish massage, you should always massage in which direction?
    a. Toward the heart.
    b. Away from the heart.
    c. Downward along the limbs.
    d. Centrifugally.

102. Is massage ever indicated during pregnancy, as long as there are not any extenuating circumstances that would otherwise be contraindicated?
    a. Yes, after the first trimester.
    b. Yes, after the second trimester.
    c. Yes, after the third trimester.
    d. Yes, during any trimester.

103. In most organs, ____ reflexes are most important in regulating visceral activities.
    a. long
    b. short
    c. cranial
    d. visceral

104. Which of the following correctly defines kinetic energy?
    a. Energy that has the potential to do work.
    b. Energy that has the capacity to perform work.
    c. The movement of an object.
    d. Energy that is doing work.

105. What is homeostasis?
    a. The internal balance of the body.
    b. The life-force of the body.
    c. An indication of disease.
    d. A condition that causes stress or strain.

106. Which of the following best defines a chronic inflammatory skin disorder where the proliferation rate of epidermal cells is accelerated?
    a. Atopic dermatitis
    b. Eczematous dermatitis
    c. Psoriasis
    d. Seborrhea

107. What does the brain stem include?
    a. Cerebrum, gyri, sulci
    b. Mesencephalon, pons, medulla oblongata
    c. Cerebrum, pons, medulla oblongata
    d. Mesencephalon, gyri, sulci

108. What is countertransference?
    a. When a client tries to personalize the therapeutic relationship.
    b. When a client tries to de-personalize the therapeutic relationship.
    c. When a practitioner tries to personalize the therapeutic relationship.
    d. When a practitioner tries to de-personalize the therapeutic relationship.

109. Which of the following are the three most common learning styles among people?
    a. Visual, auditory, tactile
    b. Visual, tactile, aesthetic
    c. Auditory, kinesthetic, solitary
    d. Visual, auditory, kinesthetic

110. Which of the following refers to the proportional limitation of a joint that is controlled by muscular contractions?
    a. Capsular pattern
    b. Hard end feel
    c. Soft end feel
    d. Contractile tissue

111. Is massage indicated or contraindicated for a client with gout?
    a. Massage is indicated during and between gout attacks.
    b. Massage is indicated only between gout attacks.
    c. Massage is always contraindicated during a gout attack, but is indicated between attacks.
    d. Massage is contraindicated during and between gout attacks.

112. What is the 5th cranial nerve?
    a. Oculomotor
    b. Trochlear
    c. Trigeminal
    d. Facial

113. Which of the following is a common disinfectant that is found in everyday use?
    a. Chlorine bleach
    b. Ethyl
    c. Cresol
    d. All of the above

114. How can massage be helpful for a client with angina pectoris?
    a. It reduces stress
    b. It decreases the effects of the sympathetic nervous system
    c. Both A and B
    d. Neither A nor B

115. What does friction do?
    a. It increases the permeability of the capillary beds
    b. It increases the amount of blood stores in the muscles
    c. It stimulates the flow of blood through the deeper arteries and veins
    d. It reduces lymphedema

116. Which barrier represents the extent of easy movement allowed during range of motion?
    a. Soft tissue
    b. Resistive
    c. Physiologic
    d. Anatomical

117. Which of the following is a mechanical effect of friction?
    a. Increased phagocytosis
    b. Reduced cerebral congestion
    c. Decreased inflammation
    d. Improved "hidebound" skins

118. Which of the following is considered a dual relationship?
    a. A person who also happens to be a massage therapist becomes a client.
    b. A client makes advances towards the practitioner.
    c. A family member becomes a client.
    d. Any therapeutic relationship between the client and the massage practitioner.

119. Why is it better to pay monthly business bills with a business check?
    a. It provides better documentation than cash.
    b. It is considered more legitimate than cash.
    c. You shouldn't use a business check; you should pay with cash.
    d. You shouldn't use a business check; you should use a personal check.

120. Which of the following is one of the major contraindications to consider before administering massage?
    a. Abnormal body temperature
    b. Acute infectious disease
    c. Inflammation
    d. All of the above

121. The term used to observe the manner in which a person walks to determine constrictions or related conditions is called:
    a. gait.
    b. gait assessment.
    c. posture assessment.
    d. observation.

122. Which of the following is not a type of boundary?
    a. Professional
    b. Personal
    c. Ethical
    d. Intellectual

123. At what point is massage appropriate on a client who has meningitis?
    a. Immediately, to help decrease inflammation of the meninges more quickly.
    b. When inflammation of the meninges has begun to subside.
    c. Not until the patient is cleared from the hospital.
    d. Never, it is postponed until the client is completely healed.

124. Which theory proves the example of briskly rubbing a part of the body that has been struck by an object to relieve the intensity of pain?
    a. Endorphin theory
    b. Nociceptor theory
    c. Gate control theory
    d. Superficial friction theory

125. Which glands secrete a watery solution that contains enzymes?
    a. Mixed exocrine glands
    b. Exocrine glands
    c. Serous glands
    d. Mucous glands

Answers and Explanations

1. D: The three classes of lymphocytes that circulate in blood are thymus-dependent T cells, bone marrow-derived B cells, and NK (natural killer) cells. T cells make up approximately 80% of circulating lymphocytes, while B cells make up 10-15%, and the remaining 5-10% is made up of NK cells.

2. D: Friction raises skin temperature by bringing more blood to the surface, thereby increasing the production of heat. This causes a 95% increase in heat dissipation. Friction encourages circulation by accelerating the flow of the blood and the lymph by emptying the veins, lymph spaces, and channels.

3. C: The primary function of ADH is to control how much water is lost through the kidneys. With the loss minimized, water absorbed from the digestive tract will be retained, which reduces the concentrations of electrolytes in the extracellular fluid. ADH release is inhibited by alcohol, which is why there is an increase in fluid excretion after consuming alcoholic beverages.

4. B: A pivot joint is a type of synovial joint that allows one bone to rotate around the surface of another bone. Synovial joints contain a joint cavity, which is the space that allows for six different types of movement. An example of a pivot joint is the atlantoaxial joint between C1 and C2; this joint allows for rotation of the head.

5. A: Cross-fiber friction is applied with the tips of the fingers or the thumb in a transverse direction across the muscle, tendon, or ligament fibers. Transverse friction is a preferable technique for rehabilitation of fibrous tissue injuries. When healing, transverse friction can promote the formation of elastic fibrous tissue and reduce the formation of fibrosis and scar tissue. This allows the healed injury to retain its original strength and liability.

6. B: Posttraumatic stress disorder is not a form of depression, but is a delayed response of intense anxiety. Some forms of depression include major depressive disorder, bipolar disorder, dysthymic disorder, postpartum depression, and seasonal affective disorder (SAD). Depression is classified as a mood or an affective disorder.

7. C: The best definition of wellness is the behaviors and habits that have a positive influence on health. It is a concept where a person takes responsibility for his state of health and makes an effort to recognize conditions, situations, and practices that may be detrimental to a healthy state. Wellness considers psychological, physical, and emotional health.

8. C: Phalanges are the small bones that make up the fingers and toes. Each finger and each toe contains three phalanges.

9. D: Assessment by palpation is both objective and subjective. Many therapists use palpation as the primary form of assessment, but it is most accurate when used in conjunction with other assessment skills. For example, with a painful condition where the pain is radiating or referred; observation and examination isolate the cause of the pain and then palpation pinpoints the source.

10. A: The brachioradialis, extensor carpi radialis longus, and extensor carpi radialis brevis all form a long mass of muscle that extends distally from the lateral supracondylar ridge of the humerus, collectively known as the "wad of three." It is just lateral to the inner elbow.

11. C: Massage is contraindicated during an exacerbation period of rheumatoid arthritis because it will worsen the inflammation that is present. When in remission, it is safe to administer massage to a client with RA. Areas and nodules that are tender should be avoided. The massage can reduce stress and gentle stretches and joint mobilizations can help increase joint mobility.

12. C: A heating pad, infrared radiation, and a sauna are all examples of dry heat. A microwave as well as a shortwave, are examples of diathermy. Diathermy is the application of oscillating electromagnetic fields to the tissue; this causes a distortion in the molecules and an ionic vibration that produces heat. Its use requires special equipment and training, and it is beyond the scope of practice of a massage therapist.

13. A: The lateral rectus muscle is innervated by the abducens nerves (VI). This pair of nerves originates in the pons and passes through the superior orbital fissures of the sphenoid bone. They are the sixth pair of extra-ocular muscles and essentially cause abduction of the eye.

14. D: Metaphase is the second stage of mitosis, which begins as the chromatids move to a narrow central zone that is called the metaphase plate. When all of the chromatids are aligned in the plane of the metaphase plate, the metaphase ends.

15. D: Maintaining visual contact, using the client's name when speaking with them, and listening attentively during the consultation are all ways of personalizing the connection between a therapist and the client. Mirroring the client's body language, voice tone, and language can also build rapport. Good rapport is the basis for trust, mutual respect, and openness that can enhance a therapeutic relationship.

16. B: Touch for health is a simplified form of applied kinesiology. Its methods are derived from both Eastern and Western origins. The purpose of this technique is to relieve stress on muscles and internal organs. Kinesiology is the principle of anatomy in relation to human movement and was developed by Dr. John Thie, D.C.

17. B: The pectoralis major muscle extends between the anterior portion of the chest and the crest of the greater tubercle of the humerus. When working on its own, it produces flexion at the shoulder joint. When working with the latissimus dorsi, it produces adduction and medial rotation of the humerus at the shoulder.

18. C: The power stroke occurs after the cross-bridge formation, during the pivoting of myosin heads. The energy to cock the myosin head is obtained by breaking down ATP into ADP and a phosphate group. In this position, the ADP and the phosphate are still bound to the myosin head. After the formation of cross-bridges, stored energy is released as the myosin head pivots toward the M line. This action is called the power stroke.

19. A: Two types of responses to pain are psychological and physical. The physical response to pain is characterized by an increase in blood pressure and pulse, and a shift in blood flow to the muscles. The psychological reaction to pain is characterized by fear, anxiety, tension, and fatigue.

20. C: A herniated disc is a protrusion of the nucleus pulposus through a tear in the annulus fibrosus. This tear can occur at the time of trauma or it can develop gradually after the trauma. This protrusion can exert pressure on the spinal nerve roots, causing pain that radiates along the path of the compressed nerve.

21. B: There are two types of isotonic contractions: concentric and eccentric. When an eccentric contraction occurs, the peak tension developed is less than the load, and the muscle elongates due to the contraction of another muscle or the pull of gravity. Eccentric contractions are common and are involved in a variety of movements.

22. C: The "objective" portion of a SOAP note includes any information gathered by the therapist during history taking, observation, and interview, as well as assessment procedures and tests. The therapist's treatment goals are also noted. Information from this objective assessment as well as data from the subjective assessment is used to design the massage session.

23. B: Lymphedema usually affects an extremity; it happens when interstitial fluid accumulates or swelling occurs in the soft tissues due to inflammation, blockage, or removal of the lymph channels. Lymphedema occurs when fluid accumulates in the interstitial spaces because it cannot pass into or through the lymph channels. A lymph drainage massage promotes the drainage of fluid accumulation.

24. A: Friction is being applied centripetally if the movement is in the same direction of the veins. The movement comes from below and travels upward; going from the hands and feet toward the body and using the thumb or palmar surface of the hand. The amount of pressure applied when utilizing friction should not be so little that the hand slips over the surface, or so great that it interferes with the movement of the blood in the arteries.

25. C: 5-8 minutes is as long as it is safe to apply friction to dry skin. It is important to take notice that skin does not become irritated by working too long without lubrication. Friction without lubrication would be effective when using the reflex effect in cases where peripheral circulation is less than optimal.

26. D: Along with increasing range of motion, massage stimulates circulation, nerve supply, and cell activity. It can also relax tense muscles and release muscle spasms. Massage can prevent or relieve stiffness and soreness of muscles and decrease the time needed to restore muscles that have been fatigued by work or exercise. The other options listed are physiological effects of massage to the skin and viscera.

27. B: Risk assessment is part of a business plan but is not included under the marketing section. Things considered when outlining the marketing portion of a business plan are descriptions of target markets and clarifications of differential advantage, a competition analysis, a strategic action plan, a marketing budget, and a summary of how marketing strategies will enable success.

28. C: A therapeutic application of deep kneading is an increase in size and firmness of weak muscles. Deep kneading is a valuable method to use in cases of paralysis and paresis, or in any case where there is tissue weakness and relaxation. Enlarged, stiffened, and painful joints may return to a normal state when inflammation is decreased.

29. B: The periosteum is the substance that covers the outer surfaces of bones. It consists of outer fibrous and inner cellular layers, but does not cover the joints. Other characteristics of bone are the

matrix, which is dense and contains calcium salt deposits; osteocytes, which are a kind of bone cells; and canaliculi, which are narrow passageways that form a branching network for exchanging of nutrients, waste products, and gases.

30. C: At least 15% of work time should be invested in marketing. Regular marketing is critical during all phases of owning and running a business, but it is also a practice that most health care practitioners neglect. It is essential to a successful business to not just rely on referrals or to slack on marketing after it is actively established.

31. B: There are two types of fibers that contribute to dermal strength and elasticity. Collagen fibers are very strong; they resist stretching but are easily bent or twisted. On the other hand, elastic fibers permit stretching and recoil to their original length. The collagen fibers limit flexibility to prevent damage to the tissue, but elastic fibers provide the tissue with some mobility.

32. C: Evidence suggests that massage was employed by the Chinese as early as 3000 years ago. It is probably one of the oldest of all forms of relief of illnesses or injuries. An ancient Chinese book called "The Cong-Fou of the Tao-Tse" was probably the foundation of both modern massage as well as the manual Swedish movements. Massage is still used extensively by the Chinese today.

33. B: To perform their functions, the kidneys rely on filtration, reabsorption, and secretion. During filtration, blood pressure forces water and solutes across the wall of the glomerular capillaries and into the capsular space. Then, solute molecules that are small enough to pass through the filtration membrane are carried by the surrounding water molecules. In reabsorption, the water and solutes from the filtrate are removed. They then move across the tubular epithelium and into the peritubular fluid. Secretion is often the primary method of excretion for some compounds; it transport solutes from the peritubular fluid, across the tubular epithelium, and into the tubular fluid.

34. D: The wellness triangle depicts the body, mind, and spirit or the physical, psychological/mental, and attitude/emotional. When all three of these aspects are healthy and in balance, a state of optimum wellness is achieved. This includes maintaining a positive mental and spiritual attitude, reducing health risks, and eliminating practices that add stress or danger to a lifestyle. Wellness is a concept in which a person takes personal responsibility for his state of health and makes an effort to recognize conditions that may be threatening or detrimental to his health.

35. D: Certain massage movements affect the blood and lymph channels in various ways. Light stroking temporarily dilates the capillaries instantaneously. Deep stroking results in a more lasting dilation and flushing of the area being massaged.

36. D: A massage session done in a spa can be as therapeutic as one done elsewhere, but it can also be challenging due to the nature of scheduling and the clients typical of a spa. Spa guests may arrive without any present complaints and do not expect much out of the massage therapy session beyond relaxation. It is also difficult for therapists to retain enthusiasm and high energy levels when under strict time constraints each day. Additionally, inexperienced clients who have not yet been educated about the effects and benefits of massage can contribute to a more challenging therapeutic massage session.

37. C: The proximal end of the first metatarsal articulates with the medial cuneiform. It is short and stocky, not long and slender like the metatarsals of toes two through five. The dorsal and medial sides are superficial and easily accessible, although its plantar surface is deep.

38. B: Kyphosis or hyper-kyphosis is an exaggeration of the normal posterior curvature (20-40 degrees) or an excessive rounding (45-50 degrees) of the thoracic spine. Characteristics of a person affected by kyphosis are a hunchback, and an apparently caved in chest with arms that tend to hang in front of the body. Rounded shoulders and a dowager's hump are also sometimes classified as mild kyphosis.

39. B: The water in the heating container should be kept between 110° and 140°F. Temperatures that are below 110°F will not be sufficiently warm enough for therapeutic application, and temperatures that are above 140°F will be difficult for the client to handle. Stones that are heated beyond this temperature may cause discomfort or even damage to the tissue if applied directly to the skin.

40. A: In pétrissage, the muscles should be lifted from the bone, and rolled and stretched in an upward direction or from the point of insertion. Whenever a muscle is grasped, it should be dragged outward from the median line at the same time. The grasp should then be released when the strain is at its maximum, which will encourage the highest degree of flow of fluids toward the parts being operated on.

41. D: A release of information form contains the client's name, the therapist's name, the name of the person(s) the information is being given to, and the time frame in which the information may be released. Files and information about the client are kept confidential unless pertinent data is being shared with the client's insurance company or other health professionals who are caring for the client. At this point, the information is only released when appropriate release of information forms have been properly signed. The completed form is signed, dated, and kept in the client's file. The only other time information from a client may be given is if it is ordered by a court of law.

42. B: Adrenal glands, which are situated on top of the kidneys, produce epinephrine, norepinephrine, and corticosteroids. These glands create the adrenaline that is most notably associated with the "fight or flight" response. Adrenal secretions give a physical and mental boost that heightens senses, sharpens reflexes, and prepares muscles when encountered with a high level of stress.

43. B: Pathology is the study of disease. Disease is a condition of abnormal function that involves anatomic structures or body systems. Diseases are characterized by signs and symptoms that are recognizable and they are typically attributed to heredity, infection, diet, or environmental factors.

44. B: Conditional contraindications require the practitioner to adjust the massage. Some techniques may cause discomfort or have adverse effects, while other therapeutic applications may still be very beneficial. It is important that the practitioner know when massage is advised and also when it should be avoided, or when specific strokes or movements should not be used. Contraindications that are absolute are not appropriate; regional or partial contraindications prohibit massage only to certain parts of the body.

45. C: The Swedish system of massage is based on the Western concepts of anatomy and physiology. It employs the traditional manipulative techniques such as tapotement, friction, vibration, pétrissage, and effleurage. It also employs additional movements that can be slow and gentle or vigorous and bracing depending on what the practitioner would like to achieve.

46. A: The vein and lymph channels are larger in the vicinity of the joints than in any other part of the limbs. This is due to the great amount of absorption that is required to keep the articulating

surfaces in good condition. This is also why joint movement and manipulation is capable of producing powerful derivative effects upon more distal parts.

47. C: A saline or salt bath should be at a temperature of 90° to 94°F and produces a tonic effect achieved by stimulating circulation. The effect of a saline bath is similar to natural bathing in sea water. The typical amount of salt used is 3-5 pounds to a tub of water and the client stays in the bath for 10 to 20 minutes.

48. C: Skeletal muscle does not include osteocytes. It is composed of muscle cells or muscle fibers, layers of connective tissue or fascia, and many nerves and blood vessels. It is the voluntary contractile tissue that moves the skeleton. Some other physical characteristics unique to skeletal muscle tissue are its striated texture, muscle fibers that have direction and can help determine the specific muscle being palpated, and the fact that it can be in a contracted or relaxed state.

49. A: A muscle or group of muscles that carries out an action is called the agonist. A muscle that has an opposite action of the agonist is called an antagonist, while a muscle that supports the agonist is called a synergist. These particular roles played by each muscle or group of muscles are necessary in order for a specific movement to occur.

50. D: Joint stretching is a powerful means of stimulation to a joint. It is a practice employed by the Turks in connection with shampooing during the Turkish bath. Stretching may be applied to the arm and shoulder joints and the finger joints.

51. B: Asclepiads was an eminent Greek physician who discovered that sleep can be induced by gentle stroking. He held the art of massage therapy in such high esteem that he refused the use of medicine of any kind and relied exclusively on massage. He claimed it produced a cure by restoring the nutritive fluids to their natural, free movement.

52. D: Deep-kneading movements should not be applied more quickly during abdominal massage. Deep-kneading movements should be applied more slowly. This allows time for movement of the fecal mass. Additionally, when performing abdominal massage, sudden thrusts should also be avoided which may cause the patient pain. Disturbances that create rigidity of the abdominal muscles will interfere with the effects of the manipulations.

53. C: The endangerment site that is at the anterior triangle of the neck is bordered by the mandible, the sternocleidomastoid muscle, and the trachea. The structures of concern at this site are the carotid artery, internal jugular vein, vagus nerve, and lymph nodes. Endangerment sites are areas of the body that warrant consideration before being massaged due to underlying anatomical structures that can be prone to injury when administering certain manipulations.

54. B: Irritable bowel syndrome (IBS) is a condition of the gastrointestinal system that involves abnormal muscular contractions. It differs from other gastrointestinal diseases in that it does not cause inflammation or any permanent damage to the intestines, nor does it increase the risk of colorectal cancer.

55. C: Massage was introduced to the Summer Olympics in 1984. Since then, sports massage has been included in every Summer and Winter Olympics. Sports massage is a type of massage that is designed to specifically enhance an athlete's performance through specialized manipulations that stimulate circulation of the blood and lymph. A team of sports massage therapists is now a regular sighting at a variety of major sporting events and sought out by many serious athletes.

56. B: Phagocytosis means "cell eating." Most cells display pinocytosis (cell drinking), but phagocytosis is performed by specialized cell-like macrophages that protect tissues by "eating" things such as bacteria, debris, and any other abnormal materials.

57. D: One of the effects of positive touch from massage is an increased level of serotonin and dopamine in the body. This can be significant because low levels of serotonin and dopamine are present in people who suffer from depression, whereas significantly higher levels are present in those with elevated moods. Positive touch can affect human physical and emotional health; it is an essential element for healthy growth and development, as supported by its ability to affect an individual's state of being.

58. D: A certification may be awarded by schools, institutions, or professional organizations to show the successful completion of courses of study or to indicate that certain qualifications have been met. It is a document that is awarded in recognition of an accomplishment or from maintaining some kind of standard. There is a National Certification Board for Therapeutic Massage and Bodywork (NCBTMB); however it does not take the place of a license where a license is required to practice massage.

59. A: Observation is a major part of the assessment process. Observation begins when the client walks in the door and continues until the client leaves the setting. A key clue to watch for at this stage is the client's body language. It will give insight to where pain and tension are being held, emotional makeup, and self-esteem.

60. D: Beta-blockers are used to treat hypertension and angina pectoris, as well as arrhythmias and migraines. They work by reducing sympathetic arousal and inhibiting the action of catecholamines at beta-adrenergic receptors. They decrease blood pressure, affect heart rate, and affect the strength of the heart's contractions.

61. D: It is important to be sure of someone's status as an independent contractor. If the IRS determines that a person hired as an independent contractor actually qualifies as an employee, you may be required to pay a heavy fine. Some characteristics that are indicative of an independent contractor status are: having the ability to pursue other clients, providing their own supplies, setting their own schedules while working no more than 20 hours per week, and clients paying them directly.

62. A: Kinesiology is the study of muscular activity and the mechanics, physiology, and anatomy of body movement. Other topics that are related to the study of therapeutic massage are anatomy, physiology, histology, and pathology.

63. B: To practice good ethics is to be concerned about your reputation, but not necessarily your own welfare. Ethics are moral guidelines that are established by professionals which aim to reduce the incidence and risk of harm or injury in the professional relationship. Without ethics, there cannot be any true professionalism.

64. D: All of the choices listed are correct. Additionally, if you want to break into a new market, you could offer introductory rates for a limited time (such as reduced rates or two-for-one deals), package deals, or a sliding scale. Before finalizing a fee structure, it is important to consider all of the costs involved in running a business, including fixed costs and amenities.

65. C: Relationship-based marketing involves truly caring about your clients' welfare. You essentially become their partner in wellness. This aspect of a therapist-client relationship is about listening, planning, educating, and being proactive and can pay off tremendously.

66. B: The seated chair massage was introduced in 1985 by David Palmer. It helped make massage more accessible to a wider range of people by making it easier to perform in a number of different places and environments. The therapist was no longer confined by heavy tables, sheets, lubricants, and the necessity for complete privacy.

67. A: The only way to document your work in a service industry is to have client files with rudimentary information included, which serves as record keeping and for the IRS. Files also need to be up to date to best inform you of your client's needs. Also, keeping updated and accurate files are necessary for insurance reimbursement, as most insurance companies will not pay for maintenance care; "reasonable and necessary" is the term used to validate a treatment modality.

68. D: Chronic is a term that refers to a lingering or ongoing condition. It is persistent or intermittent over a long period of time, often dull, diffused, and many times does not have an identifiable cause or source. It can be used to refer to pain or illness. If an illness is chronic, it progresses slowly, is difficult or impossible to remedy; and may last weeks, months, years, or be lifelong.

69. B: End feel is the feeling the therapist senses when passively moving a limb to the limit of its range of motion. The quality of this end feel indicates the presence, type, and severity of lesions in the tissues that are associated with the joint. Springy end feel is the most common; an example of springy end feel is hip flexion or extension.

70. D: Informed consent is an ongoing process. Multiple, regular sessions may require the creation of an updated care plan that includes anticipated outcomes, possible side effects, number and duration of sessions, and specific modalities. When the updated plan is finished, it is again discussed with the client and can then be signed indicating continued informed consent.

71. D: Both naproxen and celecoxib are examples of NSAIDs. NSAIDs are medications that are used most often for pain and inflammation. They have pain-reducing (analgesic) and fever-reducing (antipyretic) qualities due to the inhibition of the synthesis of prostaglandins, which are associated with inflammatory responses.

72. D: If a client tries to sexualize a massage therapy session, whether it be through sexual comments, overt advances, or requests for sexual favors, it is appropriate to state that you are uncomfortable with the comments and intentions made by the client and to terminate the session. You can then instruct the client to dress and leave, and then promptly exit the room. It should be documented what took place and what actions were taken.

73. A: Innervation is the distribution of nerves to a region of the body or a particular organ. There are nerves in the body that control specific muscles or muscle groups. There are cranial nerves that originate in the brain and pass through the foramina of the skull. There are also spinal nerves which connect to the spinal cord and pass through the intervertebral foramina.

74. D: Carcinoma originates in the epithelial tissue that lines the organs and body cavities. Sarcoma originates in supportive and connective tissues such as muscles, cartilage, and bone. Lymphoma originates in the lymphatic tissue while myeloma originates in the bone marrow. Another type of

cancer is leukemia, which originates in tissues that form blood cells. The types of cancer are determined by the kind of tissue where the cancer cells originate.

75. B: "Smith Massage Clinic" sounds less suggestive and will be perceived by potential clients in a much different way than "Smitty's Massage Parlor". Other ways to help improve the reputation of your clinic is to keep regular business hours as opposed to late-night hours, and to ensure that proper draping techniques are being used.

76. D: If the business plan is being used to secure a loan, a section titled "references" should be included, which will list all pertinent information regarding your current lending institution and the names, addresses, and phone numbers of your attorney, accountant, and business consultant. Information added to the executive summary portion should include the type of business loan(s) you are seeking and a summary of the proposed use of the funds. The financial analysis portion should specify the loan requirements and the purpose of the loan. A cover page, table of contents, and appendix are already included in a regular business plan.

77. B: It is not a national requirement for massage therapists to be licensed in the United States. Approximately two-thirds of the states require licenses for practicing massage therapy, but the definition, educational requirements, and scope of practice all vary depending on the state. While the majority of states show some basic agreement regarding the need to license massage therapists, there are many differences in defining the purpose, object, procedures, and educational requirements. This results in an undefined scope of practice for massage therapy, although it is still important for massage practitioners to recognize and practice within their legal and professional boundaries.

78. A: In the initiation stage, you introduce yourself, establish rapport, discuss general issues and expectations concerning the client, describe what you can do, and review policies and procedures. This helps improve treatment results and satisfaction by knowing what the client expects from you.

79. B: Possession of profits is actually one of the main advantages of sole proprietorship, along with ease of formation, control of all decisions, and more simple financial record keeping. A major way that a sole proprietorship varies from other business structures (corporation, partnership, LLC) is that you and your business are one entity from a legal standpoint. With this in mind, you cannot be treated as an employee of a business.

80. B: You should first identify the problem to determine if it is truly an ethical problem, then clarify the problem by gathering relevant information and define the specific type of ethical breach. Following those steps, describe what action should be taken by mapping out the best way to resolve the issue and then identify who should take action. Discussing the topic with a colleague or engaging in peer supervision are two methods for clarification.

81. B: The resistive barrier, also called the pathological barrier, is the first sign of resistance to a movement. It is important when assessing and treating soft tissue conditions. It is one of three types of barriers that can be considered when testing range of motion, the other two being a physiologic barrier and an anatomical barrier.

82. C: A practitioner/client relationship exhibits a power differential by its inherent nature. The client seeks the knowledge, skill, and authority from the practitioner's services, putting the practitioner in a place of power to provide actions or services that enhance the well-being of the more vulnerable client. During a session, the client literally looks up to and submits to the

manipulations of the practitioner. During the entirety of a session, the practitioner is often active while the client is predominately passive.

83. B: Local massage is contraindicated for 72 hours after an initial injury. Massage would worsen the pain and inflammation present after a whiplash injury. Other symptoms associated with whiplash include headaches, neck pain, limited neck mobility, difficulty swallowing, and pain radiating down the arm.

84. C: Fast fibers, which make up most of the skeletal muscle fibers in the body, are large in diameter and contain densely packed myofibrils, large glycogen reserves, and few mitochondria. Muscles that are dominated by fast fibers produce powerful contractions because the tension from a muscle fiber is directly proportional to the number of myofibrils present.

85. D: Fungi are parasitic organisms that grow in wet or damp environments. They are found mostly on the skin and mucous membranes of humans. Fungal infections such as athlete's foot, ringworm, *Candida*, and vaginal yeast infections tend to resist treatment. Molds and yeasts are also considered fungi.

86. A: "Scope of practice" defines the rights and activities legally acceptable according to the licenses of a particular occupation or profession, and an individual's scope of practice is directly related to the skills she has gained and the training she has received. In addition to particular skills and training, an individual's scope of practice is also influenced by personal limitations like belief systems, personal bias, preferred clientele, physical stature, and endurance. Many occupations and professions, including massage therapy, have national or state regulatory boards that define and enforce adherence to a scope of practice.

87. A: "Interpersonal space" refers to the actual space maintained between the client and practitioner during interactions that take place before and after the actual massage. Creating this appropriate space means maintaining a physical distance that makes both parties feel comfortable. It is important to carry on conversations at eye level whenever possible and to complete most of the conversation before the client lies down on the table. This minimizes the power differential and shows respect and consideration to the client.

88. B: It is acceptable to sell products at your place of business that are designed to assist in pain relief and promote well-being. Ethical sales of products are based on educating your clients about the products and allowing the opportunity to purchase them from you. Only products that you know to be reliable and that are a natural extension of your business are appropriate to sell.

89. C: Contractile tissues are fibrous and have tensions placed on them during muscle contractions. Contractile tissues include muscle tissue, tendons, and muscle attachments. This is one of the core concepts used in assessing range of motion, as developed by Dr. James Cyriax. The other concepts are inert tissues, end feel, and capsular pattern.

90. D: All of the options listed are valid reasons to seek supervision during a session. Some other reasons a practitioner may request that supervision take place are: having a client who is difficult or controlling; managing difficult or confusing situations that arise, sensing disappointment or ill will related to a client, or working with a client who may have been physically or sexually abused. Additionally, the practitioner should seek supervision after crossing a professional boundary with a client, when confronted with mutual or separate attraction; or when strong feelings toward a client exist, whether they are positive or negative.

91. B: Long, relaxing massages affect the autonomic nervous system by sedating the sympathetic nervous system and stimulating the parasympathetic nervous system. This results in reduced blood levels of epinephrine and norepinephrine, reduced heart rate and blood pressure, and an increased relaxation response.

92. A: Pétrissage is not a type of stimulating massage. Examples of stimulating massage techniques are vibration, which stimulates the peripheral nerves and nerve centers; percussion, which increases nervous irritability (strong percussion for a short period excites nerve centers directly while prolonged percussion anesthetizes local nerves); and friction, which stimulates nerves.

93. D: All of the above options are true. You should always carry a lot of business cards with you wherever you go and keep extras in your car or purse. You should be generous with your promotional materials in order to best circulate them; always hand out at least three business cards per person. You should also keep the card simple and not turn it into a brochure. Business cards must appeal to your target market. An effective card will convey the major benefits in a quick glace so that the client is not overwhelmed by the amount of information.

94. D: When assessing passive movement, pain and limitation in all directions usually involves the whole joint and indicate capsulitis or arthritis. Passive movement findings such as this one indicate the condition of the inert or non-contractile tissues. Limitation and pain at this point are an indication of some sort of dysfunction.

95. C: The number of speeding tickets acquired does not affect a massage practitioner's licensing status. Other reasons that can affect a license being revoked, canceled, or suspended are: being guilty of fraud or deceit in obtaining a license; practicing under a false or assumed name; being addicted to narcotics, alcohol, or other substances that interfere with duties; being willfully negligent in the practice of massage so as to endanger the health of a client; prescribing drugs or medicines without a physician's license, and ethical or sexual misconduct with a client.

96. A: In skeletal muscles, some of the motor units are constantly active, even when the muscle itself is not contracting. These contractions do not produce enough tension to cause movement, but do tense and firm the muscle. The resulting resting tension in a skeletal muscle is called muscle tone. If a muscle has little muscle tone, it appears limp and flaccid. If a muscle has moderate muscle tone, it appears firm and solid.

97. B: The acronym TART stands for texture, asymmetry, range of motion, and tenderness. Texture describes the feel of superficial and deep tissues, which may include taut bands, adherent tissue, hypertonic tissues, or flaccid tissues. Asymmetry in body structure is observed by a rotation, a curve, or a bilateral inconsistency in the body structure. Range of motion considers the quality of movement, end feel, and restricted or excessive range. Tenderness or pain is in an area or in specific tissues that may be provoked when palpated.

98. C: Planning is a stage that the client and the practitioner create with each other. In this stage, long-range treatment plans are made and are key to maintaining clients who receive treatments on a regular basis. The long-range treatment plans serve as a reminder for the client to take responsibility for his goal. It also gives both parties the opportunity to see the effectiveness of the treatment plan.

99. D: The main purposes for licenses and permits are to raise revenue and to protect the health and safety of the public. Before opening up a business, it is imperative to be aware of the local

zoning requirements. This can be a difficult process because each locale has different zoning laws and it is not always clear which department issues the various permits necessary.

100. C: In a third-class lever system, a force is applied between the resistance and the fulcrum, where speed and distance traveled are increased at the expense of effective force. A third-class lever is the most common in the body; there are few first or second-class levers.

101. A: In Swedish massage, you should always massage towards the heart (centripetally). This means that movements should be directed upward along the lower parts of the body and limbs, and then downward from the head. This facilitates the flow of venous blood and lymph back toward the heart and other eliminatory organs.

102. D: Massage is safe during all trimesters as long as the pregnancy does not have any extenuating circumstances rendering it otherwise unsafe (such as symptoms of miscarriage or being classified as high risk). However, there are some techniques that should be avoided, such as deep connective tissue and myofascial release techniques, as well as putting sustained pressure in areas that are reflexology points associated with the uterus or ovaries.

103. A: Long reflexes are the most important in regulating visceral activities in most organs. Exceptions to this are the digestive tract and its associated glands; here, short reflexes provide most of the control and coordination needed for normal functions. All visceral reflexes are polysynaptic and are either long or short reflexes.

104. D: Kinetic energy is the energy of motion; it is energy that is doing work. Energy is the capacity to perform work, but movement or physical change cannot occur unless energy is provided. Kinetic energy is one of the two major types of energy that can cause movement or physical change; the other major type is potential energy.

105. A: Homeostasis is the internal balance of the body. The body strives to maintain this balance and is affected by any changes in the stresses that are posed by an external environment. These changes require the body to constantly compensate to maintain this delicate balance.

106. C: Psoriasis is a chronic inflammatory skin disorder where the skin renews itself every few days instead of every month. Since old skin cells do not slough off fast enough, they build up in thick patches. Psoriasis typically affects the scalp, elbows, knees, back, chest, and buttocks. Approximately 1-3% of the population has psoriasis and about 30% of people with it will develop arthritis.

107. B: The brain stem includes the mesencephalon, the pons, and the medulla oblongata. The mesencephalon is the midbrain, which contains nuclei that process visual and auditory information. The pons connects the cerebellum to the brain stem and contains nuclei involved with somatic and visceral motor control. The medulla oblongata relays sensory information to the thalamus and to other portions of the brain stem.

108. C: Countertransference occurs when the practitioner personalizes a therapeutic relationship by unconsciously projecting characteristics of someone from a former relationship onto a client. It often involves misperceptions and is usually subconscious but always detrimental to the therapeutic process. The opposite of this is called transference, which is what happens when a client negatively or positively personalizes a therapeutic relationship by subconsciously projecting characteristics of someone from a former relationship onto the massage practitioner.

109. D: The three most common learning styles among people are visual, auditory, and kinesthetic. Most people use all of these methods to process information, but one is usually dominant. People with visual learning styles tend to view the world in pictures and talk a little faster than average; people with auditory learning styles prefer to discuss things and are sensitive to noisy distractions; kinesthetic learners usually speak more slowly and like to touch items and experience sensations.

110. A: The capsular pattern refers to the proportional limitation of any joint this is controlled by muscular contractions. It is one of the concepts developed by Dr. James Cyriax that are invaluable when assessing range of motion. His system tests all of the joints to isolate lesions in the hard and soft tissues.

111. A: Massage can be indicated during and between gout attacks. Massage should be postponed if the client is experiencing fever or nausea during an attack period, but may be performed if those symptoms are not present as long as the affected joints are avoided. Massage is always indicated between attacks, unless other unrelated circumstances that result in contraindication are present.

112. C: The trigeminal nerve is the fifth cranial nerve. It is the largest cranial nerve and is classified as a mixed (motor and sensory) nerve. It is responsible for providing sensation to the face as well as supporting certain motor functions of the face and jaw, such as chewing. The trigeminal nerve branches into three parts: the ophthalmic nerve, the maxillary nerve, and the mandibular nerve.

113. D: All of the above. Common household disinfectants such as chlorine bleach are effective for disinfecting linens, implements, and surfaces. Ethyl is a type of alcohol that when used as a disinfectant, destroys most types of bacteria and viruses on surfaces. Cresol is another type of disinfectant that may be combined with other products to kill bacteria, viruses, and parasites.

114. C: Massage can reduce stress in cases of stable angina. It can also decrease the effects of the sympathetic nervous system, which holds partial responsibility for coronary artery constriction. However, it is important that clients have their necessary medications with them in the event of an angina attack during a treatment session.

115. A: Certain massage movements affect the blood and lymph channels in various ways. Along with increasing the permeability of the capillary beds, friction also hastens the flow of blood through superficial veins and increases the flow of interstitial fluid, which creates a healthier environment for cells.

116. C: The physiologic barrier is within the anatomic barrier and represents the comfortable end of soft tissue stretch during range of motion. It is the extent of easy movement allowed during passive or active movements. Along with restrictive barriers, it reflects conditions of bind and ease that is related to contractile muscle tissue and fascia.

117. A: A mechanical effect of friction is encouragement of phagocytosis due to the acceleration of circulation by aiding venous and lymph circulation. When friction is being used for this purpose, it should be applied alternately to the affected part and also to the tissues between it and the heart.

118. C: A dual relationship is any situation that combines the therapeutic relationship with a secondary relationship. The secondary relationship extends beyond the normal massage practitioner/client relationship. This may arise when someone the practitioner knows becomes a client, such as a family member, friend, work associate, or someone from the practitioner's church or other organization. It is also considered a dual relationship when services are being bartered.

119. A: It is better to pay monthly business statements with a business check because it provides better documentation than cash. It is also more ideal than using a personal check. It is acceptable to use a personal check occasionally; just post the expense under Petty Cash, note which account was used, then write a check to "petty cash" for the same amount to cash. It is best to create a separate identity for personal and financial reasons.

120. D: All of the choices listed are major contraindications to consider before administering massage. Normal body temperature ranges from 96.4°F to 99.1°F. Massage is not recommended when the temperature exceeds 99.4°F; massage would tend to work against the defense mechanisms of the body. Massaging a client with an acute infectious disease would intensify the illness as well as expose the therapist to the infection. Acute inflammation in a particular area is contraindicated because massage could further intensify the inflammation.

121. B: Gait is a pattern or manner of walking; it is similar to assessing posture but it takes place with the body in motion. Gait assessment is observing this manner. The client's gait should be viewed from the front, back, and both sides. It is done as the client does a relaxed walk for several times back and forth in front of the therapist.

122. C: Professional boundaries lay the foundation for an ethical practice. Respecting personal boundaries and maintaining professional boundaries ensures that the therapeutic relationship will be healthy for the client and will be void of ethical dilemmas. Boundaries can be professional, personal, physical, emotional, intellectual, and sexual; they are personal comfort zones that help maintain a sense of comfort and safety.

123. D: For a client with meningitis, massage should be postponed until the client has healed completely. Meningitis is usually caused by viruses or bacteria and is characterized by a severe headache, fever and chills, light sensitivity, a hyperextended stiff neck, and a red spotty rash. Vertigo, nausea, projectile vomiting, mental disorientation, and seizures may also occur as the condition progresses.

124. C: Gate control theory states that painful impulses are transmitted along small-diameter and large-diameter nerve fibers that run from nociceptors to the spinal cord and then to the brain. Stimulation of thermoreceptors or mechanoreceptors by rubbing, massaging, or icing is transmitted through the larger fibers, which suppress pain sensations at the gate where fibers enter the spinal column.

125. C: Serous glands secrete a watery solution that contains enzymes. An example of serous glands is the parotid salivary gland. Serous glands are a type of exocrine gland, along with mucous glands and mixed-exocrine glands. These exocrine glands are categorized by the types of secretions that they produce.

Practice Test #2

Practice Questions

1. Which circulatory structure is described as being responsible for the carrying of deoxygenated blood centripetally to the heart by way of valves to act against gravity?
   a. Arteries
   b. Veins
   c. Interstitial fluid
   d. Lymph

2. Which answer correctly names the three parts of the small intestine?
   a. Ilium, Ischium, pubis
   b. Ileum, Ischium, cecum
   c. Ileum, duodenum, cecum
   d. Ileum, duodenum, jejunum

3. The adrenal medulla is responsible for the conversion of amino acids into ____.
   a. T3 and T4.
   b. Epinephrine, norepinephrine, and dopamine.
   c. Aldosterone and testosterone.
   d. Oxytocin and vasopressin.

4. The most superficial layer of the epidermis is the ____.
   a. Stratum lucidum.
   b. Stratum corneum.
   c. Dermis.
   d. Stratum granulosum.

5. The following answer that is NOT associated with the lymphatic system is/are the ___.
   a. Spleen.
   b. Lymph nodes.
   c. Pituitary gland.
   d. Thymus gland.

6. The stationary end of a muscle is referred to as the _____.
   a. Insertion.
   b. Origin.
   c. Antagonist.
   d. Protagonist.

7. Which of the following describes the action of smooth muscle?
   a. Striated and voluntary
   b. Striated and involuntary
   c. Nonstriated and voluntary
   d. Nonstriated and involuntary

8. How many cranial nerves make up the peripheral nervous system?
    a. 12
    b. 11
    c. 13
    d. 15

9. The _____ is/are NOT a part of the nervous system.
    a. Brain
    b. Spinal cord
    c. Heart
    d. Sensory receptors

10. _____ is/are an automatic response used to diagnose nervous disorders and also to help maintain homeostasis.
    a. Reflexes
    b. Spasms
    c. Cramps
    d. Pain

11. The _____ plexus is responsible for nervous innervation to the upper extremities and certain neck and shoulder muscles.
    a. Lumbar
    b. Sacral
    c. Cervical
    d. Brachial

12. The two systems of the body that bring oxygen to the cells and eliminate carbon dioxide from the cells are the _____ and _____ systems.
    a. Respiratory and integumentary
    b. Circulatory and integumentary
    c. Respiratory and circulatory
    d. Circulatory and nervous

13. The _____ muscle is responsible for the act of inspiration and exhalation during normal breathing.
    a. Diaphragm
    b. External intercostals
    c. Internal intercostals
    d. Transversus abdominis

14. Which of the following is not part of the axial skeleton?
    a. Parietal bone
    b. Sternum
    c. Humerus
    d. Sacrum

15.___ are responsible for the eyes' black and white vision in dim light.
   a. Cones
   b. Rods
   c. Lens
   d. Corneas

16. What is the tubelike structure that carries urine from the kidney to the bladder?
   a. Ureter
   b. Glomerulus
   c. Islets of Langerhans
   d. Urethra

17. Which of the following does NOT describe a function of blood?
   a. Transports oxygen, carbon dioxide, nutrients, and waste
   b. Regulates pH, body temperature, and osmolarity
   c. Regulates hormones
   d. Creates clots and combats toxins

18. Which digestive hormone promotes secretion of gastric juices and is responsible for motility?
   a. Secretin
   b. Oxytocin
   c. Epinephrine
   d. Gastrin

19. The place at which bones meet is defined as a
   a. suture
   b. joint
   c. aponeurosis
   d. intersection

20. The main purpose of synovial fluid is to
   a. provide lubrication
   b. promote clotting
   c. promote muscle contraction
   d. excrete through the skin to maintain homeostasis

21. Flexing the elbow exhibits active movement for the following muscle:
   a. Triceps brachii
   b. Deltoid
   c. Latissimus dorsi
   d. Biceps brachii

22. How would passive range of motion (ROM) best be described?
   a. A client moves the requested part himself
   b. A client moves against the therapist at his request
   c. A client stays still
   d. A client's body part is moved by the therapist

23. The following pathology is defined as fluid buildup from a lack of drainage in the lymph system:
   a. edema
   b. psoriasis
   c. dermatitis
   d. melanoma

24. What documentation is required to work inside a client's mouth?
   a. Signed history and release from the client
   b. Signed history and release from the client and verbal approval from the client
   c. Signed history and release from the client and verbal approval from his doctor
   d. Signed history and release from the client and written approval from her doctor

25. Which massage technique should be avoided when a client reports hypertension on their history form?
   a. Tapotement
   b. Centripetal strokes of any kind
   c. Centrifugal strokes of any kind
   d. Pressure touch

26. Pertaining to piriformis syndrome, which nerve is entrapped by the piriformis and other deep lateral rotators?
   a. Pudendal
   b. Sciatic
   c. Femoral
   d. Radial

27. When assessing a client complaining of chondromalacia patellae, the following group of muscles should be taken into consideration during treatment:
   a. Quadriceps
   b. Hamstrings
   c. Glutes
   d. Anterior compartment of the leg

28. Which of the following is NOT a cranial bone?
   a. Maxilla(e)
   b. Sphenoid
   c. Parietal
   d. Occipital

29. With what pathological condition is it absolutely contraindicated to perform massage therapy?
   a. Heart attack
   b. Skin cancer
   c. Congestive heart failure
   d. Psoriasis

30. Using light to moderate pressure with a rapid side-to-side motion is known as the technique of:
   a. Tapotement
   b. Pétrissage
   c. Pressure touch
   d. Vibration

31. When is it appropriate to begin visually assessing the client?
    a. As soon as the client walks in the door
    b. After the client has given their history
    c. After the client has gotten on the table
    d. Before the client has used the restroom

32. An individual muscle cell is called a(n):
    a. Leukocyte
    b. Adipocyte
    c. Myocyte
    d. Amino acid

33. The following occurs in the blood when heat is applied to the skin:
    a. Vasodilation
    b. Vasoconstriction
    c. Swelling
    d. Hypertension

34. Which of the following is NOT correct pertaining to the physiological effect that massage therapy has on muscles?
    a. Muscle tone is improved
    b. Muscle elasticity is improved
    c. Weak and tight muscle function is improved
    d. The temperature of the muscle is decreased by up to 1ºC.

35. Which of the following massage techniques is most commonly known for the movement of cellular waste from the muscles due to increased circulation?
    a. Pétrissage
    b. Effleurage
    c. Tapotement
    d. Touch

36. The following statement is true of the benefits of massage:
    a. The nervous system is stimulated
    b. The rate of breathing is decreased
    c. Trauma of any kind is decreased
    d. Decreases inflammation

37. Which one of the following statements is *false* regarding the physiological effects of massage of the muscular system?
    a. Increases healing time of strains
    b. Decreases scar tissue
    c. Increases range of motion
    d. Reduces pain and swelling

38. Which is the correct classification for drugs defined as illegal, with no medical use, and a high potential for addictive behavior?
    a. Schedule 1
    b. Schedule 2
    c. Schedule 3
    d. Schedule 4

39. Which areas should a massage therapist not massage when a client reports a broken wrist?
    a. Affected wrist and hand
    b. Affected wrist only
    c. Affected hand only
    d. Affected forearm and wrist

40. Which of the following roots means "kidney?"
    a. Nephro -
    b. Pulmo -
    c. Neuro -
    d. Histo-

41. The term "endoscopy" means which of the following?
    a. The use of a machine to obtain a live camera feed of the inside of the body
    b. The use of a machine to obtain a live camera feed of the outside of the body
    c. The use of an x-ray machine to obtain an image of the inside of the body
    d. The use of a magnetic resonance imaging (MRI) machine to obtain a live feed of the outside of the body

42. Which one of the four signs listed below indicates an inflammatory response in the body?
    a. Heat, redness, pain, swelling
    b. Heat, pain, swelling, fever
    c. Fever, swelling, hemorrhage, redness
    d. Pain, swelling, fever, hemorrhage

43. During muscular contraction, the action potential is created by activating voltage-gated sodium channels down the axon toward the
    a. Voltage-gated channels
    b. Calcium channels
    c. Neuromuscular junction
    d. Acetylcholine receptors

44. Adenosine triphosphate (ATP) binds to which of the following during muscle contraction to release actin?
    a. Troponin
    b. Tropomyosin
    c. Actin
    d. Myosin

45. With regard to skeletal muscle, which of the following neurons travel from the muscle to the spinal cord during contraction?
    a. Motor neurons
    b. Muscle spindle cells
    c. Sensory neurons
    d. Golgi tendon organs

46. The rectus femoris' main actions are to
    a. Flex the hip and flex the knee
    b. Flex the hip and extend the knee
    c. Extend the hip and extend the knee
    d. Extend the hip and flex the knee

47. The insertion of the biceps brachii is located on the
    a. Ulnar tuberosity
    b. Humerus at the lateral supracondylar ridge
    c. Radial styloid process
    d. Radial tuberosity

48. The massage technique that can be used to increase heat production is called
    a. Kneading
    b. Stroking
    c. Vibration
    d. Stretching

49. Which of the following is a physiological effect that massage has on the integumentary system?
    a. Skin losing pallor
    b. Stimulation of sebaceous glands
    c. Decreased perspiration
    d. None of the above

50. Which one is NOT an example of an acute athletic injury?
    a. Dislocations
    b. Infections
    c. Contusions
    d. Sprains

51. Which actions does the elbow make when actively moving through the normal range of motion?
    a. Adduction/abduction
    b. Flexion/extension
    c. Inversion/eversion
    d. None of the above

52. A client complains of pain in his leg. He is unable to flex his knee. Which muscle or group of muscles is most likely affected?
    a. Quadriceps
    b. Gastrocnemius
    c. Biceps brachii
    d. Hamstrings

53. Which of the following is a contraindication for touch?
   a. Numbness
   b. Burns
   c. Headache
   d. None of these

54. Which of the following massage techniques is beneficial for treating jaundice?
   a. Tapotement
   b. Pressure touch
   c. Friction
   d. Reflex stroking

55. Friction would be contraindicated for which condition?
   a. Edema
   b. Sprains
   c. Sciatica
   d. Varicose veins

56. Centripetal friction should be performed in all of the following pathologies EXCEPT
   a. Arthritis
   b. Pain
   c. Gout
   d. Edema

57. Which of the following is NOT a contraindication for joint movement?
   a. Synovitis
   b. Fracture
   c. Ankylosis
   d. Rheumatoid arthritis

58. Joint pain can be relieved by all of the following EXCEPT
   a. Pressure
   b. Movements of the joint above
   c. Massaging the area above the affected joint
   d. Massaging the area below the affected joint

59. A client complains of anxiety from a recent stressful life event. Which stroke should not be used for the client's benefit?
   a. Stroking
   b. Pétrissage
   c. Kneading
   d. Percussion

60. Which of the following is NOT an absolute contraindication for massage?
   a. Shock
   b. Kidney failure
   c. Hemorrhage
   d. Arthritis

61. An indication for using cold hydrotherapy is
    a. Cold hypersensitivity
    b. Compromised superficial circulation
    c. Strain
    d. Heart attack

62. Which of the following is within the therapist's scope of practice to determine whether massage therapy is indicated for any client?
    a. Taking a pulse/blood pressure
    b. Checking his or her blood sugar
    c. Performing an oral examination
    d. All of the above

63. The kneading technique described as using the heel of the hand or the whole palmar surface is
    a. Pétrissage
    b. Digital
    c. Palmar
    d. Effleurage

64. To perform centripetal friction to the leg, the therapist would move
    a. From the ankle to the patella
    b. From the patella to the ankle
    c. From the patella to the hip
    d. From the hip to the patella

65. Chucking is a useful massage technique to treat
    a. Insomnia
    b. Headache
    c. Paralysis
    d. Tetanus

66. Which of the following is not a form of percussion/tapotement?
    a. Cupping
    b. Hacking
    c. Wringing
    d. Beating

67. During the application of massage, which technique should be alternated with friction?
    a. Wringing
    b. Joint movement
    c. Vibration
    d. Kneading

68. When performing joint movement:
    a. Stabilize the distal portion of the limb
    b. Move the proximal portion of the limb
    c. Shake the distal portion of the limb
    d. Stabilize the proximal portion of the limb

69. The shifting of fluids from one part of the body to another is known as
    a. Hydrophobia
    b. Osmosis
    c. Hydrostatic effect
    d. Hydrophilia

70. Which of the following would provide the most stimulation?
    a. Application of a heat pack
    b. Application of a cold pack
    c. A hot bath
    d. None of the above

71. The acronym "RICE" means
    a. Rest, ice, constrict, elevate
    b. Rest, ice, compression, exercise
    c. Rest, ice, compression, elevation
    d. Rest, ice, constrict, exercise

72. Which of the following is an indication for heat therapy?
    a. Strain
    b. Bleeding
    c. Contusion
    d. Fever

73. When applying cold to a client, which of the following is true?
    a. It decreases metabolism
    b. It increases circulation
    c. It increases metabolism
    d. It decreases muscle tone

74. The site where the muscle fiber and nerve fiber meet is known as the
    a. Neurotransmitter
    b. Aponeurosis
    c. Joint
    d. Neuromuscular junction

75. Which term best describes a sudden involuntary contraction of a muscle or group of muscles that does not cause pain?
    a. Spasm
    b. Reflex
    c. Cramp
    d. Constriction

76. Which of the following terms is also known as "muscle testing?"
    a. Passive movement
    b. Active movement
    c. Assisted movement
    d. Resisted movement

- 44 -

77. For support of the client, bolsters may be positioned under the client's _____ when prone and under the _____ when supine.
    a. Ankles, knees
    b. Ankles, neck
    c. Ankles, lower back
    d. Hips, knees

78. The appropriate temperature of a massage room is between
    a. 60 and 66ºF
    b. 72 and 78ºF
    c. 75 and 80ºF
    d. 68 and 74ºF

79. Which of the following may occur after a relaxation massage session?
    a. Slight headache
    b. Bruising
    c. Decreased urine output
    d. Decreased appetite

80. Which psychological pathology cannot be directly treated by massage therapy?
    a. Depression
    b. Insomnia
    c. Anxiety
    d. Schizophrenia

81. Which term is defined as the stage at which a therapeutic massage strategy is being determined and therapeutic modalities are selected?
    a. Performance
    b. Evaluation
    c. Planning
    d. Assessment

82. The purpose of a code of ethics is to
    a. Provide principles of correct and incorrect conduct
    b. Provide informed consent from a client
    c. Provide principles of good and evil
    d. Provide personal prejudices to place on the race and religion of clients

83. Which best describes how a therapist should follow ethical behavior?
    a. The therapist should conduct all actions and activities within the law
    b. The therapist should conduct all actions and activities within their best judgment
    c. The therapist should conduct all actions and activities within their scope of practice
    d. The therapist should conduct all actions and activities within their professional image

84. When is it ok to discuss a client's information with someone else?
    a. It is never ok to discuss a client's information with anyone
    b. It is ok to speak with the client's spouse and immediate family
    c. It is ok to speak with the client's friends
    d. It is always ok to discuss a client's information with anyone

85. How do ethics differ from laws?
    a. Ethics do not carry any punishment
    b. Laws do not carry any punishment
    c. Ethics may be punished in a variety of ways including fines, licensure revocation, and criminal trial
    d. Ethics violations are measured by degrees and can be punished by fines, probation, and community service

86. A professional boundary can be best described as
    a. The space of the client in a therapeutic relationship
    b. The space of the therapist in a therapeutic relationship
    c. The physical, emotional, and spiritual space between the client and therapist
    d. None of the above

87. In which of the following environments would it be the most difficult to maintain professional boundaries?
    a. The therapist's home
    b. The client's home
    c. The therapist's office
    d. The restroom

88. What word defines the personalization of a therapeutic relationship?
    a. Misconduct
    b. Countertransference
    c. Interpersonal communication
    d. None of the above

89. When a client asks the therapist out on a date in the massage session, what is the BEST way to handle the situation?
    a. The therapist should stop the massage and tell the client to leave
    b. The therapist should stop the massage and explain that if they were to go on a date, the therapist would have to first refer the client to another therapist and then they can begin a personal relationship
    c. The therapist should answer and then continue the massage
    d. The therapist should answer and then stop the massage

90. Which type of dual relationship is NOT acceptable?
    a. A therapist and client trade massages because the client is also a therapist
    b. A therapist and client are dating and have been engaging in sexual activity
    c. A therapist and client are business partners
    d. A therapist and client are friends and attend a spinning class together

91. Ethical behavior includes all of the following EXCEPT
    a. Legally acceptable behavior
    b. Boundaries
    c. Scope of practice
    d. Confidentiality

92. The study of morals, values, and principles is defined as
    a. Scope of practice
    b. Legal compliance
    c. Moral compliance
    d. Ethics

93. Which of the following is NOT out of the scope of practice for a therapist?
    a. Using electrical stimulation to excite/relax muscles
    b. Performing therapy inside the mouth with a prescription
    c. Telling a client to drink water
    d. Performing internal massage to the sacrococcygeal ligaments

94. When is it ok to tell a client to drink water?
    a. It is not ok; it is outside the scope of practice for a massage therapist
    b. It is ok after the treatment
    c. It is ok anytime
    d. It is ok only before the treatment

95. Which of the following is the correct way to abbreviate the credentials of a licensed massage therapist?
    a. Dr. Jane Doe, LMT
    b. Mrs. Jane Doe, LMT
    c. Jane Doe, Ph.D., LMT
    d. Jane Doe, LMT, DO

96. Which of the following is NOT a personal hygiene guideline that should be practiced by a therapist?
    a. Brush teeth and use mouthwash when appropriate
    b. Keep hair fresh and styled appropriately so long hair does not touch the client
    c. Take time for relaxation and physical fitness
    d. Eat fast food when possible

97. Which of the following is the best definition of the word "virus"?
    a. Minute, unicellular microorganisms that have both plant and animal characteristics
    b. Parasitic microscopic agents that are capable of transmitting disease between organisms
    c. Eukaryotic microorganism that contains chitin in their cellular walls
    d. None of the above

98. Which of the following is considered the most effective safety practice to prevent the spread of disease?
    a. Showering
    b. Laundering sheets
    c. Washing hands
    d. Vacuuming

99. A substance that prevents infection by the killing of bacteria is known as a
    a. Disinfectant
    b. Sanitizer
    c. Sterilizer
    d. None of the above

100. What is the percentage of bleach solution used to clean up a spill of bodily fluids?
     a. 5%
     b. 10%
     c. 15%
     d. 20%

101. Where is the best place to store client records?
     a. File folder
     b. File folder inside of a box
     c. File folder inside of a locked box
     d. They can be placed anywhere

102. Having a home-based business has several advantages. Which is NOT an advantage?
     a. No commute
     b. Family members disrespecting boundaries
     c. Be your own boss
     d. Make your own schedule

103. Which of the following is a disadvantage of being self-employed?
     a. Independence from employers
     b. Do not have to worry about commission
     c. Can have employees
     d. Financial risk

104. What is the length of time that confidential client records are kept?
     a. 1 year
     b. 5 years
     c. 8 years
     d. 10 years

105. Outlining a business' purpose, setting goals, and stating an objective are known as
     a. Financial planning
     b. Presenting
     c. Business planning
     d. Accounting

106. Whose work was craniosacral therapy based on?
     a. W. G. Sutherland
     b. John Harvey Kellogg
     c. Mark F. Beck
     d. None of the above

107. Which of the following can be considered objective information?
     a. Pain level assessment
     b. Duration of pain
     c. Client goals
     d. Range of motion (ROM) testing

108. Where would the therapist document what the client has expressed?
    a. Subjective
    b. Objective
    c. Assessment
    d. Plan

109. Which of the following can be defined as a client interview, history, visual observation, and palpation with range of motion?
    a. Observation
    b. Performance
    c. Planning
    d. Assessment

110. During an assessment, what is comparing one side of the body to the other known as?
    a. Unilateral symmetry
    b. Bilateral symmetry
    c. Balanced symmetry
    d. None of the above

111. Which of the following results of a muscle test should be referred to a doctor?
    a. Weak and painless muscle test
    b. No strength in the muscle
    c. Strong and painless muscle test
    d. Weak and painful muscle test

112. Assessing how the client walks and carries herself is known as
    a. Gait assessment
    b. Postural assessment
    c. Bilateral assessment
    d. Quadrilateral assessment

113. Which of the following conditions cannot be treated with massage?
    a. Tachycardia
    b. Atrophy of the heart muscle
    c. Myocarditis
    d. None of the above

114. Which of the following is the correct treatment order for carpal tunnel?
    a. Release muscles, increase range of motion (ROM), decrease pain
    b. Decrease pain, increase ROM, release muscles
    c. Increase ROM, decrease pain, release muscles
    d. Only the fascia should be worked

115. Why is it important to get a verbal intake?
    a. The client may have forgotten to write something on their form
    b. It is faster than a written intake
    c. It takes less time
    d. None of the above

116. Which of the following is NOT a massage therapy modality?
    a. Reiki
    b. Jiu-jitsu
    c. Thai
    d. Polarity therapy

117. A client complains of numbness and tingling down her left arm. What should the beginning treatment plan include?
    a. Left neck, shoulder, arm, and wrist
    b. Left neck
    c. Left neck and shoulder
    d. Left neck and arm

118. During a massage, the therapist feels a warm and red raised area on the client's arm. There is no wound, but the client expresses that it is painful. What is this area most likely?
    a. Tumor
    b. Infection
    c. Inflammation
    d. Contusion

119. What is the belly of a muscle referred to in the Shiatsu method of massage therapy?
    a. Hiro
    b. Hara
    c. Hilot
    d. None of the above

120. Which client position is best for on-site corporate massage events?
    a. Prone
    b. Supine
    c. Seated
    d. Standing

121. Which method of massage therapy was developed by Boris Chaitow and Stanley Leif to relieve compressed nerves that refer pain to other parts of the body?
    a. Polarity therapy
    b. Reiki
    c. Neuromuscular therapy
    d. Shiatsu

122. The focus of applied kinesiology is
    a. Strengthen and tone muscle tissue
    b. Emotional release
    c. Increasing structural balance and functionality
    d. Meditation and relaxation

123. During a relaxation massage session, a client is expressing that his pain is unbearable. What is the best course of action?
a. Ignore him
b. Tell him to relax
c. Ease off the pressure, and ask him if his pain has decreased
d. Tell him it is part of the massage

124. When checking range of motion (ROM) on a client, the therapist notices limited flexion in her knee. Which muscle(s) should be addressed?
a. Quadriceps
b. Hamstrings
c. Adductors
d. Glutes

125. Upon bilaterally comparing the client's calves, one side is much more firm than the other. This can be due to all of the following EXCEPT
a. Hypertonicity
b. Overuse
c. Postural/gait Imbalance
d. Nerve damage

Answers and Explanations

1. B: The answer arteries is incorrect because they are the structure responsible for carrying blood away from the heart. Interstitial fluid is incorrect because it is the fluid between cells and tissues, not responsible for moving at all. Lymph is incorrect because it is made up of the white blood cells and immune cells. It is not a structure that is used to move blood.

2. D: Ilium, Ischium, pubis are incorrect because these are the bones of the pelvis. Ileum, Ischium, cecum are incorrect because the ischium is part of the pelvis, and the cecum is part of the large intestine. Ileum, duodenum, cecum are incorrect because the cecum is part of the large intestine.

3. B: T3 and T4 are incorrect because these hormones are made in the thyroid gland. Aldosterone and testosterone are incorrect because the adrenal cortex and testosterone is produced in the gonads. Oxytocin and vasopressin are incorrect because these hormones are made in the pituitary gland.

4. B: The stratum lucidum is incorrect because this is the layer only present in the thick skin of the fingers and the soles of the feet. Dermis is incorrect because the dermis is the layer of skin containing collagen and elastic fibers. Stratum granulosum is incorrect because this is the middle layer of the epidermis.

5. C: Spleen is incorrect because the spleen is the largest lymph tissue in the body responsible for phagocytosis. Lymph nodes are incorrect because the lymph nodes are part of the lymph system and hold lymph in places throughout the body. The thymus gland is incorrect because it is part of the lymph system because it provides the site for the maturation of T cells.

6. B: Insertion is incorrect because it is the moving end of a muscle. Antagonist is incorrect because the antagonist is a muscle that performs the opposite action to another muscle. Protagonist is incorrect because the antagonist is a muscle that performs a similar action to another muscle

7. D: Striated and voluntary are incorrect because they describe skeletal muscle. Striated and involuntary are incorrect because they do not describe any muscle fibers of the body. Nonstriated and voluntary are incorrect because they do not describe any muscle fibers of the body.

8. A: There are 12 cranial nerves: olfactory, optic, oculomotor, trochlear, trigeminal, abducens, facial, vestibulocochlear, glossopharyngeal, vagus, spinal accessory, and hypoglossal.

9. C: The brain, spinal cord, and sensory receptors are incorrect because they are part of the nervous system.

10. A: Spasms are not correct because spasms do not assist with maintaining homeostasis, nor are they solely used to diagnose nervous disorders. Cramps are not correct because cramps do not assist with maintaining homeostasis, nor are they solely used to diagnose nervous disorders. Pain is not correct because pain does not assist with maintaining homeostasis, nor is it solely used to diagnose nervous disorders

11. D: Lumbar is incorrect because the lumbar plexus innervates the legs, genitals, and parts of the abdomen. Sacral is incorrect because the sacral plexus innervates the glutes, perineum, and parts of the legs. Cervical is incorrect because the cervical plexus innervates the skin and muscles of the head and neck, cranial nerves, and diaphragm.

12. C: Respiratory and integumentary is incorrect because the integumentary system is not responsible for any type of cellular respiration. Circulatory and integumentary is incorrect because the integumentary system is not responsible for any type of respiration. Circulatory and nervous is incorrect because the nervous system is not responsible for any type of respiration.

13. A: External intercostals are incorrect because the external intercostals' action is to push air out of the lungs during abnormal breathing, like breathing deeply. Internal intercostals are incorrect because the internal intercostals' action is to assist the diaphragm by pulling air into the lungs during deep breathing. Transversus abdominis is incorrect because this muscle's action is to compress the abdomen.

14. C: Parietal bone is incorrect because this skull bone is part of the axial skeleton. Sternum is incorrect because the sternum and ribs are part of the axial skeleton. Sacrum is incorrect because this bone is part of the axial skeleton, along with the other vertebrae.

15. B: Cones are incorrect because cones are responsible for seeing color and visual acuity. Lens is incorrect because this anatomical structure focuses the light for clear vision. Corneas are incorrect because these anatomical structures refract light.

16. A: Glomerulus is incorrect because this is a functional structure of the kidney. Islets of Langerhans are incorrect because this is a functional structure of the kidney. Urethra is incorrect because this is the tube structure from the bladder to the external body that carries urine for elimination

17. C: Regulates hormones — this is correct because the blood does not regulate hormones; this is the function of the endocrine system. Transports oxygen, carbon dioxide, nutrients, and waste is incorrect: this is a function of blood. Regulates pH, body temperature, and osmolarity is incorrect, this is a function of blood. Creates clots and combats toxins are incorrect, these are a function of blood.

18. D: Secretin is incorrect because secreting promotes the secretion of bicarbonate. Oxytocin is incorrect because oxytocin plays a role in childbirth. Epinephrine is incorrect because epinephrine is released during times of stress.

19. B: Suture is not correct because a suture is a "stitch" of bone. Aponeurosis is not correct because this is a layer of tendons. Intersection is not correct because it is not an anatomical term.

20. A: Synovial fluid is only used to lubricate joints and to reduce the amount of friction between moving bones. It does not promote clotting, which is part of the circulatory system. Muscle contraction is performed by myocytes, and sebaceous glands are responsible for excretions through the skin.

21. D: The triceps brachii extend the elbow. The deltoid does not attach at the elbow; it moves the shoulder. The latissimus dorsi also does not attach at the elbow; it moves the arm.

22. D: Active movement is when a client moves the part on their own. Resistive movement is when the client moves against the therapist, and no movement is made when the client stays still.

23. A: Psoriasis is a skin disorder due to skin cells dying too rapidly. Dermatitis is an inflammation of the skin. Melanoma is a type of skin cancer.

24. D: It is mandatory to obtain not only a prescription from the client's doctor for inside her mouth because without this document, it is outside the scope of practice for a therapist to perform massage inside the mouth. It is also mandatory for a therapist to obtain a written history and release from the client prior to any therapeutic treatment.

25. B: Centripetal strokes should be avoided because the strokes are made toward the heart, increasing blood pressure and stressing the client's circulatory system.

26. B: The sciatic nerve runs between the body of the piriformis and the gluteus muscles. The pudendal nerve is just lateral to the sacrum, but it is not associated with piriformis syndrome. The femoral and radial nerves are located in the leg and arm, respectively.

27. A: The quadriceps should be addressed because the patella is encased in the tendon of the quads. This would be most beneficial because releasing and stretching the quadriceps would provide the most benefit regarding pain and range of motion compared to the hamstrings, glutes, and anterior compartment of the leg.

28. A: Maxilla(e) is correct because the sphenoid, parietal, and occipital bones are cranial bones.

29. C: Massage therapy is absolutely contraindicated in patients with congestive heart failure because of the slow disease process with the heart muscle becoming weaker and weaker. Any type of massage therapy can prove detrimental, and it can even kill the patient. A heart attack and skin cancer client can be massaged using careful consideration with regard to techniques, as well as written consent from their doctor. Psoriasis is not contraindicated, unless the patient experiences pain or has open sores.

30. D: Tapotement is a type of percussion, with the hands repetitively striking the skin. Pétrissage is a kneading motion. Pressure touch is the placement of the hands with light pressure on the skin.

31. A: It is appropriate to assess the client as soon as they walk in the door because the therapist can gauge their natural gait, posture, and any other indications of neuromuscular imbalance.

32. C: A leukocyte is a white blood cell. An adipocyte is a fat cell. An amino acid is a building block of proteins, and it is a collection of organic atoms bonded together.

33. A: Vasoconstriction is caused when cold is applied to the skin. Swelling can be possible when heat is applied, but it is not directly correlated with heat application. It is also a cause of vasodilation. Hypertension is a slight effect of when cold is applied to the skin.

34. A: During massage, the myocytes are never enlarged. Blood can flow through the muscle more easily, but the tone of the muscle is not affected.

35. A: Effleurage, tapotement, and touch do not have an effect on circulation.

36. B: The nervous system can be stimulated or repressed, trauma is usually decreased, and inflammation may or may not be affected by massage.

37. A: Massage decreases the healing time of strains, decreases scar tissue, increases range of motion, and reduces pain and swelling.

38. D: Schedule 4 drugs are classified as illegal, and all the other schedule drugs are not.

39. A: It is important to only work on the part proximal to the injured part because manipulating the part below can be painful for the client, or this can cause longer healing times.

40. A: Pulmo- means lung, neuro- means nerve, and histo- means liver.

41. A: Endo- means inside and -scopy means scope.

42. A: Pain, fever, and hemorrhage are not always present with inflammation.

43. C: The neuromuscular junction is where nerves meet muscle and where the action potential is carried for contraction. Mitochondria are the energy powerhouses of cells. Calcium channels play a part in action potentials, but they do not receive the action potential. Acetylcholine receptors receive acetylcholine, but not action potentials.

44. D: Troponin is attached to the protein tropomyosin during muscle contraction. Actin and myosin slide past each other during muscle contraction.

45. C: Motor neurons run from the spinal cord to the skeletal muscle to control voluntary muscle contraction. Muscle spindle cells are sensory receptors in the belly of a muscle. Golgi tendon organs are sensory receptors in the tendon to detect when and how much a muscle is being stretched.

46. B: The rectus femoris originates at the anterior inferior iliac spine and inserts at the aponeurosis in the patella. The muscle covers two joints; it flexes the hip and extends the knee.

47. D: The biceps brachii inserts at the bicipital aponeurosis and the radial tuberosity.

48. A: Kneading is correct because the muscle is picked up off of the muscle, manipulated, and placed back again on the muscle. Stroking does not create any heat because it is simply a nervous stimulation of the superficial skin. Stretching does not create any heat when the muscles are stretched. Vibration creates some heat due to the muscle being manipulated laterally, but it does not create any significant amount of heat.

49. B: Skin losing pallor and decreased perspiration are not physiological effects of massage on the integumentary system. Skin reddening and increased perspiration, as well as stimulation of the sebaceous glands are a few physiological effects of massage on the integumentary system.

50. B: Infections are not an acute athletic injury because there is not one specific incident that causes an infection that can be determined as the trauma. An infection takes time to develop, but dislocations, contusions, and sprains do not.

51. B: The elbow is a hinge joint and only has two actions — flexion and extension.

52. D: The hamstrings are responsible for flexing the knee and extending the hip. The quadriceps flexes the hip and extends the knee. The biceps brachii flexes the forearm and supinates the arm. The gastrocnemius dorsiflexes the foot.

53. B: Burns are a contraindication for touch because they are extremely sensitive to touch. Touching a client with burns can cause pain and cause increased healing time for the patient.

54. C: Friction assists with the treatment of jaundice because friction moves blood more quickly through the body by increasing circulation and promoting cellular waste movement. This technique will help the client's body to remove the excess bilirubin from the blood through the kidneys and reduce jaundice.

55. D: Friction is contraindicated for varicose veins because the veins are no longer properly working, and friction can increase the amount of varicose veins that a client has. Friction is beneficial for edema to drain fluid. Friction can decrease the healing time of strains, and it can improve blood flow to the muscles in the lumbar spine to treat sciatica.

56. C: Gout is the buildup of uric acid in the joints, and when centripetal friction is used, this can cause the uric acid to move to other joints and worsen the condition. Arthritis, pain, and edema will lessen with friction due to the improvement in circulation and elimination of cellular waste from the tissues.

57. D: Joint movement for rheumatoid arthritis (RA) is beneficial because it can increase the synovial fluid around the joint and bring nutrients to it, decreasing inflammation. Synovitis, fractures, and ankylosis are all immobilizing conditions, and the joints in, on, or around them should not be moved to reduce the risk of increased pain and healing time.

58. D: Massaging the area below the affected joint would not be beneficial because the area above may be manipulated inadvertently so that the pain in the joint above is increased.

59. D: Percussion is a stimulating technique to the nerves of the body, while stroking, pétrissage, and kneading are all sedative. Any type of neurological disorder derived from stress should use sedative techniques during treatment.

60. D: Arthritis is not a contraindication for massage because joint movement and other techniques are beneficial to reducing the inflammation of arthritis. Shock, kidney failure, and hemorrhage all add a risk of death to the client if he or she is massaged during acute and even chronic phases of these pathologies due to the fluctuation in blood pressure, increase in circulation, and cellular waste in the bloodstream.

61. C: A strain can be treated with cold hydrotherapy because of the vasoconstrictive properties that can reduce inflammation. Cold hydrotherapy should not be used in cases of cold hypersensitivity, compromised superficial circulation, or heart attack because these pathologies would worsen immediately or cause a delayed response, worsening the condition.

62. A: Taking a pulse/blood pressure is correct because the other three procedures are out of the scope of practice of a massage therapist.

63. C: Palmar kneading uses the palm of the hand, pétrissage and effleurage use the whole hand, and digital kneading uses only the fingers to perform the technique.

64. A: "Centripetal" means toward the heart or from inferior to superior in most cases.

65. D: Tetanus is the rigidity of a muscle. Chucking is useful to "reset" the muscle spindle cells to allow the muscle to relax. Cupping, hacking, and beating are percussive movements that may cause the muscle to tense up more.

66. C: Wringing is a type of kneading. Cupping, hacking, and beating are all forms of percussion.

67. D: Friction should always be alternated with kneading to promote the movement of cellular waste out of the body.

68. D: If the proximal portion of the limb is not stabilized, stress will be placed on any joints proximal to the joint that the therapist is working on, possibly causing pain. This will also inhibit joint movement.

69. D: Hydrophobia is the fear of water, and hydrophilia is the love of water. Osmosis is the movement of cellular molecules in a solvent from an area of lower concentration to a higher concentration.

70. B: Cold hydrotherapy is generally stimulative, and heat is generally sedative. To remember this, think of how you feel in a cold shower versus a warm shower.

71. C: Rest means to rest the injured part by keeping it immobile as much as possible. Ice means to ice it regularly to reduce inflammation and promote healing. Compression means to wrap or bandage the area to prevent infection or bruising. Elevation means to keep the injured part at or above the heart to promote draining of inflammation and cellular waste.

72. A: Bleeding, contusion, and fever are all contraindications for heat therapy because they can worsen with heat. Strains are indicated for heat because the heat vasodilates the blood vessels and allows for freshly oxygenated blood to rush in and promote healing.

73. A: Cold decreases the metabolism due to vasoconstriction. Heat therapy increases circulation and metabolism. Exercise increases muscle tone.

74. D: A neurotransmitter is a form of communication between nerves, an aponeurosis is where several tendons meet, and a joint is where two bones meet.

75. A: A reflex is a sudden movement of a muscle due to outside stimulation. A cramp is like a spasm, but the client feels pain as well. Constriction is not a medical term for any condition.

76. D: Passive movement is when the therapist moves the body part for the client. Active movement is when the client moves the body part for the therapist. Assisted movement is when both the therapist and the client move the body part together.

77. A: The client should have any joints that flex toward the table supported when supine, as well as prone. Some clients also prefer their neck supported when supine for this reason.

78. B: According to the Ohio State Medical Board and the *American Massage Therapy Association (AMTA)* ethics, the room temperature should be between 72 and 78ºF.

79. A: During any massage session, the client should not have any bruising. The client may have a slight headache, increased urine output due to the cellular waste in the bloodstream, and increased

appetite due to massage therapy's sedative properties that activate a client's parasympathetic nervous system.

80. D: Schizophrenia cannot be directly treated by massage because it is a psychological condition that cannot be treated by activating the client's parasympathetic nervous system, as can be done with depression, insomnia, and anxiety.

81. C: Planning is also the P in SOAP notes. Assessment is determining which pathological and neuromuscular conditions are present. Evaluation can be categorized as taking a history and learning subjectively and objectively about the client. Performance is not a part of massage therapy's strategies.

82. A: Although informed consent and principles of good and evil can be considered a part of ethics, it is not the purpose of ethics. Personal prejudices are considered unethical.

83. C: It is very important that the therapist put their scope of practice first as their guidelines for all behavior. Because ethics are always lawful, the therapist will most always be following the law. Unfortunately, a therapist's best judgment and professional image are not always ethical, and they should not be considered when following ethical behavior.

84. A: It is both unethical and a violation of HIPAA to discuss a client's information with anyone but the client.

85. C: Although laws are harsh, ethical issues are often more detrimental because they can tarnish a therapist's reputation and cause other difficulties. Laws do not take ethics into consideration and usually only have monetary or time-serving-type penalties.

86. C: A professional boundary includes not only the space of the client and therapist, but the emotional and spiritual space as well. A client can violate one boundary without violating the others.

87. B: The client's home is the most difficult environment in which to maintain professional boundaries because the client's home is usually more of an informal environment and the client has the "power" to direct the session how they'd like to if the therapist does not exhibit himself as a professional practicing within his scope.

88. B: Misconduct is the unethical behavior of a therapist. Interpersonal communication is the written, verbal, or otherwise means of conveying a message to another.

89. B: A therapist should NEVER start a dual relationship in session and should always communicate with the client as clearly and nicely as possible, while making sure that the client understands. It is also imperative to explain the scope of practice and to convey oneself as an ethical professional.

90. B: This is an example of a dual relationship that is unethical due to the absence of boundaries between client and therapist.

91. A: Legally acceptable behavior is not always concurrent with ethical behavior. In the eye of the law, a therapist can break a law while acting ethically: Some may argue that Dr. Kevorkian, who

assisted patients with committing suicide, was acting ethically, but he also broke the law by being an accomplice to murder.

92. D: Scope of practice is a set of rules drawn out to clearly define what a medical professional can and cannot do. Legal compliance is simply following laws. Moral compliance is simply following one's own morals.

93. B: Telling a client to drink water is out of the scope of practice because this is telling a client what to do in terms of ingestion. Internal massage is not in the scope of practice, except in the mouth with a written prescription from a doctor. Electrical stimulation is only in the scope of practice of chiropractors and physical therapists.

94. A: Telling a client to drink water is out of the scope of practice because this is telling a client what to do in terms of ingestion.

95. B: Jane Doe does not have any other medical license or credentials, so it is never appropriate to put Dr., Ph.D., or DO anywhere in her name.

96. D: A therapist's diet is their choice, but it is not a hygienic guideline to eat fast food when possible.

97. B: Answer A describes bacteria, and answer C describes a fungus.

98. C: Although showering, laundering sheets, and vacuuming are good safety practices, hand washing is proven to be the number one way to prevent the spread of germs.

99. A: A sanitizer kills germs and bacteria but not all bacteria. A sterilizer is also a cleaner, but it is more widely used to kill bacteria on surfaces.

100. B: According to the State Medical Board of Ohio and the Federation of State Medical Boards (FSMB), the correct percentage solution is 10%.

101. C: According to the Federation of State Medical Boards (FSMB), all confidential client information should be organized in a locked box or filing cabinet.

102. B: No commute, being one's own boss, and making one's own schedule are great advantages of a home business. Family members not respecting boundaries is one of the drawbacks of this setup.

103. D: Independence from employers, no longer worrying about commission, and the possibility of having employees are great advantages of being self-employed, but there is a high level of financial risk involved.

104. D: Per the Federation of State Medical Boards (FSMB), the minimum amount of time a therapist should keep their confidential client records is 10 years.

105. C: Financial planning, presenting, and accounting are all subsets of business planning.

106. A: John Kellogg invented massage therapy; Mark Beck is an author who worked from Kellogg's massage information.

107. D: Range of motion (ROM) testing is objective because it is information that is observed by the therapist. Pain level assessments, duration of pain, and client goals are subjective because only the client can determine this information.

108. A: Subjective is what the "subject" has told the therapist. Objective is what "objects" the therapist has found. Assessment is the determination of pathologies and neuromuscular conditions, and plan is a treatment strategy for the session.

109. D: Observation, performance, and planning are not specific to each piece of information being obtained by therapist.

110. B: Bilateral means both sides, and symmetry is defined as similarity from one side to the other. Unilateral means one side, and balanced symmetry does not allude to comparing one side of the body to the other.

111. D: A weak and painful muscle test could describe a serious sprain or strain that may need to be operated on, or it is a symptom of a neurological issue. A weak and painless muscle test arises from atrophy. A strong and painless muscle test is normal, and no strength in the muscle can also be from atrophy.

112. A: Postural assessment is more likely to describe when a client is standing still. A bilateral assessment is comparing each side of the body against the other. Quadrilateral assessment is not a term used in massage therapy.

113. C: Myocarditis is not treatable with massage therapy because the heart cannot directly or indirectly be treated to reduce the inflammation of the pericardial sac. Tachycardia can be treated with any centrifugal and/or sedative techniques. Atrophy of the heart muscle can be treated with several sessions of light centripetal strokes.

114. A: It is important to first release any hypertensive muscles to make way for effective stretching to then increase range of motion. Pain should always be last on a therapist's task list because pain is subjective and just because a client feels less pain does not mean that a muscle has been released or that the functionality of the area has increased.

115. A: It is always important to discuss the massage therapy session and review the client's history before beginning treatment, because the client almost always has a more elaborate explanation regarding their goals. This always gives the therapist the opportunity to ask questions and get more specific information not obtainable on a brief history form.

116. B: Reiki, Thai massage, and polarity therapy are all common modalities in massage therapists are trained. Jiu-jitsu is a Brazilian martial art.

117. A: It is important to treat the client's entire left upper extremity, including the neck, because it may be difficult to determine where the nerve impingement is originating.

118. C: The four signs of inflammation are redness, swelling, heat, and pain.

119. B: Hara is the belly of a muscle in Shiatsu massage.

120. C: Because corporate massage events are most often held in offices, it is best for the clients to be seated, due to the professional atmosphere and lack of time that the clients may have. They also do not have to be concerned about disrobing.

121. C: Reiki was developed by Usui in Japan in the early 1900s. Polarity therapy was developed by Randolph Stone, D.O., D.C., N.D. Shiatsu was developed by the Japanese before early civilization.

122. C: The focus of exercise is to strengthen and tone muscle tissue. The purpose of Touch for Health and other energy therapies is for emotional release. A variety of therapies, not including applied kinesiology, have a focus on meditation and relaxation.

123. C: It is important to be in communication with the client and to make him feel as comfortable as possible. Ignoring him will not build trust and is rude. Telling the client to relax is to not reciprocate the communication between client and therapist, and it can also prevent a trusting professional relationship. Telling him it is part of the massage is also inconsiderate and will not build trust.

124. A: The quadriceps are the group of muscles that extend the knee, and during a range of motion test, they can be indicated as being hypertonic if there is limited flexion of the knee joint.

125. D: Nerve damage does not change the size of a muscle with regard to bilateral comparison. Hypertonicity, overuse, and postural/gait imbalance are all possible outcomes of one side exhibiting a firmer touch.